Maureen Axf

BECKENHAM

To Maureen,

Eric Inman

Beckenham's coat of arms.

BECKENHAM

Eric Inman
&
Nancy Tonkin

Phillimore

2002

Published by
PHILLIMORE & CO. LTD
Shopwyke Manor Barn, Chichester, West Sussex

ISBN 1 86077 206 4

Printed and bound in Great Britain by
BOOKCRAFT LTD
Midsomer Norton, Bath

Contents

To Robert Borrowman, G.W. Tookey, Q.C., and H. Rob. Copeland,
whose enthusiasm for the history of Beckenham
has inspired us to write this book.

List of Illustrations

Frontispiece: Coat of Arms

Illustration Acknowledgements

Mrs Joyce Ayling, 77; Beckenham Cemetery, 49; Beckenham Theatre Centre Ltd, 154, 155; Borrowman, 4, 14, 16, 37, 51, 108, 115; British Museum, 126, 127; Mr R.E. Castle, 95; Christ Church, 116; Copeland Collection, 45, 50, 58, 59, 68; Croydon Advertiser Group, 148; Crystal Palace Foundation, 38; Mrs V. Davis, 149; Mr John Gent, 40, 102; Mr Andrew Hajducki, 18; Miss A.M. Hayes, 76; Mr Charles Hooper, 147; Miss Eileen Howard, 48; Hulton Deutsch Collection, 136; Dr Eric Inman, 1, 2, 46, 52, 55, 80, 90, 107, 114, 156, 157; Mrs Eileen Jenner, 158; Kent Fire Brigade Museum, 44; Mr R.Larg, 57, 94, 122, 131; London Borough of Bromley, 125, 153; London Borough of Bromley Local Studies Library, 23, 49; London Transport Museum, 63; Mr Kenneth Miller, 54, 55; Milne Electrical Collection, Chalk Pits Museum, Amberley from *The Electrical Review* for January 1901, 48; *Motor Sport*, 64; Muirhead Vactric Components Ltd, 104; Mrs Irene Mulry, 75; Phillimore & Co. Ltd, 3; Mr R.C. Riley, 150; Mrs Olga Roberts, 147; J Sainsbury Plc, 152; St George's Church, 151; Mr John Summerville-Meikle, 120; Syndication International, 43; Tookey Collection, 60, 93; Mr Ray Webb, 138; Mrs Betty Wiseman, 139; The remaining 88 illustrations are from the Nancy Tonkin Collection.

Acknowledgements

Sadly, this revised edition cannot be the work of both original authors as Nancy Tonkin unexpectedly died two years after its first publication. It would be impossible to do full justice to the contribution which Nancy made to this history. A true Beckenhamian, born and bred, she had a vast fund of knowledge of the area and a tireless enthusiasm for everything she undertook. Fortunately, her husband Bill has agreed to help with the revisions for this edition and has made available her postcard collection for the illustrations, where needed. We hope this will continue to be both the definitive history of Beckenham and a fitting memorial to an outstanding lady and historian.

A work of this nature would be impossible without the assistance of many people and organisations, of whom we would particularly like to mention the following:

Mr Simon Finch, Senior Librarian of the Bromley Local Studies Library for his help and advice. Andrew Hajducki for allowing us to see his unpublished book entitled 'The Railways of Beckenham' and permitting us to reproduce an illustration. Mr A. J. Harris (Beckenham Cemetery & Crematorium) for pointing out the positions of graves and allowing us to see the cemetery archives. Mr Len Hevey for reading the manuscript and his helpful comments. Mrs Jo Inman for proof reading and correcting the manuscript. Mr A.C. Johns for permission to reproduce illustrations from the Copeland Collection. Mrs Pat Manning for giving us access to her researches on the Cator family. Mrs Mary McInally for information on Minshull School and St Edmund's. Miss Pam Notcutt for advice on planning aspects. Mr R.C. Riley for information and advice on railway matters. The Diocese of Rochester for providing information on the modern parish boundaries. Mrs R.S. Tookey for permission to reproduce illustrations from the Tookey Collection.

Inevitably some will have been overlooked. To them we express our apologies and trust the end result will be sufficient compensation for their effort.

Introduction

Our definition of Beckenham is the former parish of St George which survived as a distinct administrative unit, with only minor boundary changes except for the addition of West Wickham in 1934, until its incorporation into Greater London in 1965.

Although only nine years have elapsed since the first edition of this book there have been very considerable changes to present day Beckenham as well as an increased knowledge of the past. We have retained the popular format of the original edition and most of the illustrations whilst revising the text so as to provide a balanced, comprehensive and up to date introduction to all aspects of the history of the town.

Beckenham extends roughly from Stumps Hill on Southend Road to the north, to West Wickham on the south, and from a point close to Bromley South Station in the east to Crystal Palace Parade to the west. What we have to remember is that these boundaries were decided when the parish consisted of a tiny country village with its associated farmsteads. Looking at early maps it is easy to see how the boundaries of the parish followed the edges of fields or the lines of rivers or streams. Three tribulets of the Thames drain the area—The Beck, The Chaffinch and The Pool.

Beckenham is now a typical outer London suburb and not an obviously historic place. There are no timber-framed buildings, no ancient fortifications, and even the parish church is a relatively modern creation. Appearances can be misleading, however, and this is particularly so in the case of Beckenham which has a long and fascinating history going back to at least the Roman occupation.

1 One of the 1868 cast iron parish boundary posts which was re-erected on Beckenham Green in 1995 to commemorate the 20th anniversary of Bromley Borough Local History Society.

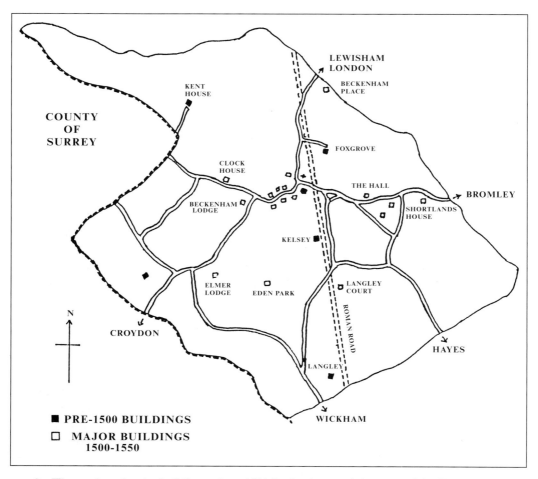

2 The roads and major buildings of pre-1550 Beckenham and the route of the Roman road.

The tongue of land stretching up to the summit of Sydenham Hill and resulting in part of Penge, and a third of the Crystal Palace grounds, being in Beckenham looks suspiciously like a later addition to the original parish. Borrowman, in his book *Beckenham Past and Present*, tells of a tradition that centuries ago an unknown corpse was found on the top of the hill where the Crystal Palace was built. According to the story, the vestry of the parish in which the body was found declined to bury it, but that of Beckenham did in return for the land on either side of the body together with that comprising the route to the church in Beckenham. This is unlikely as the strip in question consisted of open pasture and did not include the road down which such a funeral party would have naturally travelled. It is much more likely that it was part of Penge Common which the owners of Kent House had acquired in the distant past.

One

The Past

Beckenham Village and Parish

The earliest known inhabitants of what is now Beckenham are believed to have arrived from the continent during the Iron Age some two thousand years ago. Traces of their fortified encampment surrounded by ancient forest are surprisingly still to be seen at the highest part of the parish near Tootswood Road. The Saxon term 'Toot' denotes a look-out, or beacon point. 'Tootswood' may have been the site of an outpost of the Iron-Age fort at Keston. This point was used in June 1887 for one of the great chain of bonfires, lit throughout the country, to commemorate Queen Victoria's Golden Jubilee. Due to the generosity of two local ladies, the Misses A.J. and W.S. Jay, of 41, South Hill Road, the site has, since 1962, been in the care of the local authority with the proviso that it is never developed. In 1885 traces of Roman pottery were found there. The original occupiers of this camp were displaced or subdued by the Roman occupation of Britain in A.D. 43. Whether any Roman or Romano-British buildings were erected in the area is purely a matter of conjecture because no significant remains have been uncovered. A Roman road leading from London to the iron workings near Lewes was constructed through the area, so it is quite possible that Roman buildings once existed and that their remains have been destroyed by later development. What happened when the Romans departed about A.D. 410 is not known but Dr Moore's pollen analysis at the Tootswood site suggests that an Anglo-Saxon settlement existed in the area round about the sixth century, possibly on the sandy well-drained land to the south of the present High Street. A recent archaeological dig conducted in this area by the Museum of London revealed only Saxon loom pits and weights but no remains of dwellings. The settlement may have been under the leadership of Beohha, the man from whom Beckenham is generally believed to derive its name. The district was well wooded, with oaks thriving on the clay soil and water meadows stretching to the Thames on the west, ideal for a small community existing by farming, hunting wild boar or deer, and by fishing in the local streams.

After the Norman Conquest, Beckenham formed part of the possessions of Odo, Bishop of Bayeux and half brother of the King. It was well settled with both a manor and a mill as is recorded in Domesday Book. The site of the manor house is almost certainly on the high ground, overlooking what was then a ford, where the Public Hall, National Westminster Bank and adjoining office building now stand in Bromley Road. Examination of the excavations for the foundations of the latter building in 1991 by one of the authors (ERI) revealed traces of a previous building, but the only artefacts recovered were a trade token and a 16th-century wine vessel. The mill was almost certainly on the stream, formerly called the Hawkes Brook, just inside what is now the main entrance to Kelsey Park.

In the reign of Edward I the manor was owned by the de la Rochelles, who came originally from France. It later passed to the Bruyns when Sir Maurice Bruyn married Matilda Rokele. Elizabeth Bruyn, a great-great grand daughter of this marriage, took William Brandon as her second husband, so that in the reign of Henry VII the manor passed to the Brandons. William Brandon was a standard-bearer at the battle of Bosworth Field, where he was slain. It is said that his son, Charles, Duke of Suffolk entertained Henry VIII on a journey to Hever to visit Anne Boleyn. The manor came into the hands of Sir Oliver St John and remained with the St Johns, afterwards Viscounts Bolingbroke, until late in the 18th century. It was sold to John Cator in 1773. The site of the manor house is almost certainly where the Public Hall and adjoining office building now stand in Bromley Road.

Further substantial houses were constructed in the parish from the 15th to the 18th centuries, such as at Foxgrove, Elmers End, Langley and Kelsey. The Elmers End site was occupied during the 13th to 15th centuries and was at one time owned by Robert de Retford, one of the king's itinerant judges. Thos. Motley's estate map of 1736 shows the unusual arrangement of two concentric moats but not the house. The area was bought in the 1860s by the Croydon Board of Health for use as a sewage farm and its moats were filled in. It was used as a sewage farm until the 1960s. Since then a large lake has been created and the site turned into a conservation area and bird sanctuary. Originally the site was partly in Beckenham but since 1997 it has been entirely in the London Borough of Croydon. There is an entrance to it from Elmers End Road opposite Dorset Road.

Anſgot de Rouec̄ teñ de eṕo *Bacheha̅*. *In Brvnlei hd̄.*
p̄ . ii . ſolins ſe defd̄ . Tra . ē . viii . car̄ . In dn̄io ſunt . ii . 7 xxii.
uilli cū . viii . bord b̄nt . viii . car̄ 7 dimid . Ibi . xii . ac p̄ti.
7 iiii . ſerui . 7 uñ mold̄ . 7 ſilua . lx . porc̄.   ẜ de rege . E..
T . R . E . 7 poſt: ualeb . ix . lib̄ . Modo: xiii . lib̄ . Anſchil tenuit

---

In BROMLEY Hundred
Ansgot of Rochester holds BECKENHAM from the Bishop.
It answers for 2 sulungs. Land for 8 ploughs. In lordship 2.
22 villagers with 8 smallholders have 8½ ploughs
Meadow, 12 acres; 4 slaves; a mill; woodland, 60 pigs.
Value before 1066 and later £9; now £13.
Askell held it from King Edward.

3   The entry in Domesday Book describing Beckenham with an English translation.

4 This photograph of the Old Manor House, taken in the 1870s, shows a basically Georgian-style building with a lower annexe attached to its northern end. From a report in the *Beckenham Journal* we know this attachment was older than the main structure. Both were demolished when the Council purchased the Manor House in 1882 for use as offices.

Foxgrove was also moated and appears to have fared somewhat better than Elmers End. In the reign of Edward III, this Manor belonged to John de Foxgrave. It seems to have changed hands quite frequently either by sale or by marriage until in the 18th century it had become part of the Langley estates, coming into the possession of Sir William Burrell in 1789. He sold it to his nephew Sir Peter Burrell IV, later Lord Gwydir. Four years later, by special Act of Parliament, it passed to the Cator family as part of a land-holding rationalisation.

The history of Kelsey and Langley is very different. The original Kelsey Mansion was built close to the site of the mill in 1408 by William Kellshule, a London fish merchant. It fell into disrepair after the Burrells built a grander mansion in 1766 further upstream facing the existing artificial lake. Originally a simple building, it was much enlarged and rebuilt in Scottish baronial style by the London banker, Peter Hoare, during his residence from 1849 to 1877. It was finally demolished in 1921.

Langley Place was a large farmstead owned by the Longele family from the 13th to the 15th centuries. During this time the Malmain family and the Violetts lived there for a period. At the beginning of the 16th century John Style, a London merchant, purchased the property and developed it into a gentleman's seat.

5   Foxgrove Farm, *c.*1870. The Manor House was demolished in about 1830 and this farmhouse erected in its place. This in turn was pulled down about 1878 and the remainder of the moat filled in to allow the estate to be developed for housing.

6   Kelsey Manor had been much enlarged and altered by the time this picture was taken. This is as it appeared after being rebuilt by the banker Peter Hoare who provided the town with its first fire station and hospital. It was demolished in 1921.

7 The Mansion at Park Langley, *c.*1910. This was the home of Sir Oliver Style of Langley who nearly doubled the size of the old parish church by adding north and south transepts with family vaults underneath during 1619-21.

On the death of Sir Humphrey Style in 1718 his daughter, Dame Elizabeth Elwill, inherited the estate. A few years later her son, Sir Edmund Elwill, sold it to Hugh Raymond, a director of the South Sea Company. On his death in 1737 the property was inherited by his son Jones Raymond. His sister, Amy, married the second Peter Burrell of Kelsey and, on the death of her brother Jones in 1768, she succeeded to the Langley estates, as well as the Foxgrove Manor. Thus the Burrells owned Langley, Kelsey and Foxgrove. On Amy's death in 1789 this vast property of over 3,000 acres went to her grandson, Peter Burrell IV, and when he died in 1820 the connection of the Burrell family with Beckenham came to an end and the properties were put up for auction. The three-day sale in October 1820 at Garraway's Coffee House included Langley Farm, Langley Lodge, Kelsey Park, Eden Farm, Stone Farm, *The Three Tuns*, Elmer Lodge and many houses and some shops in the village. Langley was purchased by the Goodhart family whilst Kelsey was bought by Edward Grosse Smith who in 1835 sold it on to the Hoares, the banking family. Both ceased to be family homes by the turn of the century.

Eden Farm was described as 'an elegant seat', the residence of William Eden who later became Lord Auckland. He entertained Pitt the Younger, Dundas, the elder Wilberforce, Vansittart, Lord Teignmouth, and other leaders of the Evangelical laity. His sister was married to Archbishop Moore of Canterbury. Eden Farm was large and easily able to accommodate the frequent overnight visitors who often totalled a dozen or more at a time. It was surrounded by superb gardens and shrubberies, with many large oak and elm trees in the grounds. The estate was open parkland covering an area almost down to Elmers End and Croydon Road. The mansion was a large white building in the classical style and stood where Crease Park is in Village Way. William Eden, 1st Lord Auckland, became Ambassador to Spain in 1787 and to the Netherlands two years later. He bought Eden Farm in 1807 but died seven years later, when he was succeeded by his eldest son George, who later became Governor General of India.

Kent House, the first house in Kent coming from the London area, stood in Kent House Road not far from its junction with Lennard Road. It was an estate in the 12th century owned by a Norman nobleman. His grandson sold it to Sir Richard de la Rochelle *c.*1246, who leased half of its value of quit rents to the hospital of St Katharine by the Tower of London. At the beginning of the 19th century it was used as a farm by James Randall and became known as Kent House Farm. The *Morning Post* in 1815 advertised the property as having Common Rights on Penge Common (see reference to 'tongue of land' in the Introduction). It continued as a farm until the turn of the century when it became first a nursing home and later a private hotel, before being demolished in 1957.

There were several other farms and lodges in the district during the 18th and 19th centuries but we have only touched on major large establishments. Farms towards the west side of the village were Elm Farm near the railway bridge in Barnmead Road and Thayers Farm nearer to Clock House Station. Copers Cope Farm, off the Southend Road, was approximately 250 acres in extent and stretched to the New Beckenham area with footpaths to Kent House Farm. The gentrified farm house on the corner of Copers Cope Road still stands there today, and is a listed building. Stone Farm was at the top of what is now Stone Park Avenue near the Chinese Garage. These farms supplied the area with milk and meat—the cows being milked and the cattle slaughtered on the premises.

8   Kent House, *c.*1890. In the 17th century the Lethieulliers occupied the house and then sold it to John Julius Angerstein. Thackeray certainly stayed there and it is believed that Samuel Pepys, who was a friend of the Lethieullier family, may well have visited the house.

9 Stone Farm seen here *c.*1910 only disappeared when Stone Park Avenue and the parade of shops was built in Wickham Road between the wars. Before the area became known as 'The Chinese Garage' it was called 'Looking Glass Corner'.

Of the more modest buildings of old Beckenham, the *George Inn*, said to be over 300 years old, is the only property in the High Street to survive to the present day. The petty sessions were once held there. Three other buildings existed long enough to be recorded by the camera. The Old Wood House, a timber-framed building of primitive basic construction stood where W.H. Smith's now stands and was demolished in the 1930s; next to it was Gordon House, pulled down to make way for the original Sainsbury's which was opened in 1915; whilst a little further on in the direction of Thornton's Corner was the so-called Manor House with its conspicuous glass-covered entrance way. Village Place, rebuilt in 1717, stood roughly opposite the entrance to the present Village Way. It was the home of the Lea-Wilsons, one of whom became Lord Mayor of London and had an extensive garden stretching behind the other High Street properties all the way to Church Hill.

Austin's pork butchers, next to the *Three Tuns* public house, was originally a gardener's cottage and said to date from at least the 17th century. It was not demolished until the 1960s after having been in the Austin family for over 100

10 *Left.* Old Wood House in the High Street, *c.*1905. This picturesque old building may have been built as a Yeoman's Hall. When it was demolished it was discovered that it had originally been one large hall with a central fireplace and only a hole in the roof to let out the smoke.

11 *Below left.* The exact age of the *George Inn* is not known but a Richard King is recorded as paying Hearth Tax there in 1662. The covered entrance way to the Manor House can be seen on the left of the picture.

12 *Right.* Austin's shop by the side of the newly rebuilt *Three Tuns* public house, *c.*1905. The lower part of the shop was of brick and stucco, and the upper part of green oak weatherboarding on timber framing. The plaster was made of straw and cow-dung.

13 *Below.* Shortlands Farmhouse, *c.*1918. This old building is reputed to have been the model for the cottage in Enid Blyton's Noddy stories.

years. Elm Cottage, which stood on the corner of what is now Village Way, was demolished in 1914 to make way for Beckenham's first cinema 'The Pavilion', and may also have been a simple timber-framed building. It was here that Borrowman the historian was born.

Other old buildings still remaining today are the cottage near the Chinese Garage, the Bailiff's Cottage in Manor Way, Langley Chapel, and the farmhouse on the corner of Shortlands and Bromley Roads.

Beckenham, unlike nearby Bromley, is not on a main road to the coast and this, together with its position, an easy ride to and from the capital, probably contributed to its growing popularity among rich London merchants as a site for a country home. The number of memorials to wealthy gentry and their servants formerly to be found in and around the parish church is one indication of this. Several references in the church records show that many of the gentry had black or coloured servants at this time. In 1715 a twice-weekly coach service from Beckenham to London points to the development of a worthwhile demand from within the parish.

The mid-17th-century hearth and poll tax returns for the parish of Beckenham have survived and, when these are compared with the first national census taken 200 years later, it can be seen that there had been a very substantial increase in population, including many wealthy people. The poll tax return contains the names of 203 people, so if we assume an equal number of children and that some of the inhabitants managed to escape the collectors, the population of the parish in 1645 must have been round about five hundred.

The interesting feature of this list—apart from the disparity of rate between that of the gentry (£10-£30) and that for the parson (1s.) and ordinary folk including wives of any status (6d.)—is that it reveals only four households of any size and that even these, including Langley, had very few servants. None of the substantial houses, which we know existed at the end of the 18th century, feature in the return. There were probably less than 100 houses in the village at that time.

This situation is confirmed by the hearth tax return made only some 20 years later. In all 52 persons were charged for 181 hearths, and 40 were non-chargeable, not possessing more than one. Hearths were difficult to conceal so the information given here is likely to be more accurate than that in the previous poll tax return. Once again a picture of a parish with relatively few very modest houses appears. Only four dwellings have more hearths than the seven of the *George Inn*, the only building surviving to the present day and which can now be seen to be fairly small. The 24-hearth dwelling occupied by John Scott is obviously Langley, the next with 12 hearths occupied by a Mr Brogrove is Kelsey whilst the other two, each with nine, are assumed to be the Old Manor House and either Foxgrove or the Rectory.

The Beckenham Old Manor House has already been referred to but, just across the road in 1789, the Rev. William Rose built his new rectory with its Adam fireplace, now to be seen in Bromley Civic Centre. The extensive garden with its vista over water and pasture was designed by the famous landscape architect, Humphry Repton, who also advised Peter Burrell at Langley whilst on a visit to Beckenham in 1790. The design of the garden is interesting for it seems to have

14 Presumably wishing to be one up on his prosperous new neighbours, the Rev. William Rose hired the Adam brothers in 1789 to design his new rectory (situated on what is now Church Avenue). The following year he invited the famous landscape architect, Humphry Repton, to advise him on the layout of the garden.

15 Clock House, *c*.1895. The well wooded gardens contained a sizeable lake with ornamental fountain and the extensive stable block was surmounted by a large clock which gave the building its name.

been copied, or inspired by, those of the Manor House, where the middle ground was occupied by lawns and a lake, or possibly by Village Place or Beckenham Lodge. Village Place we know was rebuilt in 1717 and its extensive grounds stretched the full length of the back of the properties on the north side of the High Street. The Beck had obviously been diverted and landscaped to accommodate the gardens of Gordon House and the other Manor House and it is interesting to speculate whether this would have been allowed to happen unless they were already in existence when the Village Place garden was laid out.

Development was not confined to the village itself. Clock House, Shortlands House, The Hall and Beckenham Place all belong to this period.

Clock House was built early in the 18th century and Sir Piercy Brett, 'Admiral of the Blue', lived there until his death in 1781. The substantial, red-brick mansion was built close to the main road from Penge to Beckenham and later the nearby railway station was to take its name from the house. Sir Piercy was followed by John Cator's brother Joseph, who lived there for thirty years after his return from India. He had six sons and several daughters. After his death, it had various tenants. The house was demolished in 1896 but the stables stayed as part of Horsman's Nursery and others, until they were finally pulled down in 1926.

Shortlands House was built at the start of the 18th century. It was here that George Grote the historian was born in 1794. For many years he was an M.P. and introduced the 1833 Ballot Bill. George Grote was offered a peerage which he refused, but on his death in 1871 he was buried in Westminster Abbey. Later Shortlands House became the residence of W. A. Wilkinson, an M.P., whose family was largely responsible for the building of St Mary's church. The grounds of the house covered over 130 acres, much of which was sold as building plots in 1863. At the auction the land realised nearly £500 per acre, an incredibly high sum for those days. Earlier last century the house ceased to be used as a private residence and became an hotel until 1950, when it was purchased by the Roman Catholic diocese for use as a preparatory school. In 1955 a secondary department was opened and three years later became a full scale secondary grammar school under the name 'Bishop Challoner School'.

16   John Cator, Lord of Beckenham Manor, belonged to the second generation of the family to live in the area, his father, also named John, having moved to Bromley in 1762. The main family residence was Beckenham Place with two subsidiary houses, Clock House on Penge (now Beckenham) Road and The Hall on Bromley Road.

By far the most influential of the 18th-century newcomers were the Cators. John Cator (1728-1806) a wealthy timber merchant whose wharf and yard was on the south bank of the Thames, a site later occupied by the Bankside Power Station, since transformed into the Tate Modern Art Gallery. He probably built Beckenham Place soon after his marriage in 1758. His father-in-law, the eminent botanist Peter Collinson F.R.S., mentions the fact in a letter dated 1761 and his residence there is recorded on a map dated 1769. In 1764 his father died in Bromley where he had retired two years earlier, thus providing him with the resources to expand, adding first

17   Beckenham Place, *c.*1890. In 1784 John Cator added the ornamental frontage which had formerly belonged to Wricklemarsh Place at Blackheath. Over the entrance is the Cator family motto, 'Nihil sine Labore' (Nothing without Work). The two statues at each side of the door have recently been recovered from the cellars and can now be seen in the visitor centre.

Copers Cope Farm, then Foxgrove Farm and finally Kent House Farm, and rapidly building up a very large estate of properties both inside and outside the parish. He purchased the Lordship of the Manor of Beckenham and the old Manor House in 1773, a title which is held by the Cator family to this day. In 1785 he succeeded in diverting Southend Road so that it did not pass too close to his new mansion. Situated at the top of Stumps Hill, it commanded a fine view over Kent and London. Two years later he added the portico from Wricklemarsh Place in Blackheath which he had bought for housing development. The family crest prominently displayed on this portico is one confirmed to William Cater, possibly no relation, in 1566. It was formally granted to John Barwell Cator in 1818. He and his wife Mary entertained a succession of famous people including the celebrated

Dr Johnson, who is on record for describing Beckenham Place as one of the finest places at which he was ever a guest. He was a frequent visitor and formed the library and catalogued it. The library is now in Woodbastwick Hall, in Norfolk, the seat of the Cators. Mrs Thrale, Fanny Burney, Sir Joshua Reynolds, and the Adam brothers all came to Beckenham Place. There seems little doubt that John Cator corresponded with the Swedish botanist Linnaeus, but it is unlikely that the latter ever visited the house or, as Borrowman relates, planted trees and shrubs in the grounds.

On John Cator's death in 1806 the estate was inherited by his nephew, John Barlow Cator, who was responsible for the acquisition in 1838 of the coat of arms now so prominently displayed on the Wricklemarsh portico. He was the last member of the Cator family to live in Beckenham Place, which had a succession of tenants until 1902 when it was occupied by a private boys' school called Craven College. In 1905 the school moved to Elmer Lodge in Beckenham and the house became the home of the Norwood Sanatorium, famous for its discrete treatment of wealthy alcoholics and drug addicts. The sanatorium had little need for extensive grounds so in 1907 they were leased to the Foxgrove Golf Club who built a club house near the Westgate Road entrance. Finally in 1928 the London County Council purchased the whole site as a green area for the extensive Downham and Bellingham estates it was developing. The sanatorium moved to Chislehurst and the mansion and grounds opened as a municipal golf course in 1934. Finally, as a result of the demise of the Greater London Council in 1977, control passed to the London Borough of Lewisham and in 1995 boundary adjustment removed the last connection with Beckenham.

Two

The Creation of Beckenham Town

The Building and Growth of the various Estates

The first Survey of 1798-9 and Pigot's 1839 *Directory of Kent* provide us with the first really detailed picture of the village of Beckenham. It straggled along the main road from what we now call Thornton's Corner to the junction with the roads to Croydon and Penge, separated from the tiny hamlet of Elmers End by open country. The Rector and the Lord of the Manor lived up the hill outside the village proper. There were no road or street names as we know them now; all the early directories simply give an address as 'the village'. Pigot tells us there were 35 tradesmen and that the nobility and gentry numbered 18. 13 years later, just before the opening of the Crystal Palace, the gentry had almost doubled to 33 and were served by 44 tradesmen. Beckenham, even at this time, was a fast-growing high-class community. This was to be dwarfed by the changes which took place soon afterwards when the proximity to London and the arrival of the railways led to the development of the area. This was to be of great financial benefit to the Cator family.

John Cator (1728-1806) and his wife Mary came to Beckenham Place in the late 1750s. They only had one child, Maria, who died when three years old. As a result, in 1806 the estate passed to John's nephew, John Barwell Cator, the eldest of the numerous children of his brother Joseph who lived at Clock House. Barwell Cator was a very different man from his uncle. Eccentric in his later years and a keen sportsman, he spent much of his time in Ireland, living only occasionally at Beckenham Place, the birthplace of his wife, Elizabeth. In 1807 he purchased Woodbastwick Hall in Norfolk, the better to pursue his sporting interests, leaving Beckenham Place to be occupied by a series of tenants. Being close to London, the development of Beckenham was inevitable but it was Barwell Cator's gambling debts which sparked off the family need to convert land into cash. In 1825 he obtained parliamentary approval to develop his estates for housing. At one time he mortgaged many of the freeholds of his properties to the Prudential Assurance Company for £187,000, a truly vast sum halfway through the 19th century.

The most important member of the Cator family concerned with Beckenham was Peter, the youngest son of Joseph, who returned from a career in the Indian Civil Service just in time to save the family fortunes. He persuaded his brother to hand over control of the Beckenham estate to his eldest son Albemarle, and to appoint himself as agent. Peter, unlike his brother John Barwell Cator, seems to have inherited his uncle's shrewdness and business sense. He lived on the estate at The Hall and took an active interest in the affairs of the parish. He sold land in 1854 for a railway on nominal terms providing trains did not run on Sundays during the time of divine service, and for housing which had to conform to strict up-market standards, with plenty of accommodation for servants, carriages and gardens. Many of these large houses have now been replaced by blocks of flats or even by small estates of town houses.

The first houses on the estate were large and detached, and had a minimum of half an acre of ground. This was later reduced to one third of an acre when the sale of the houses slowed down. The roads on the Cator Estate were unmade and owners of the properties had to pay a fair share of the expense of maintaining and keeping in good and substantial repair the roads, footpaths and water drains. They were charged according to the footage of the road frontages of the houses. These regulations also covered walls and fences surrounding the property. Most of the houses were built with stabling and coach houses.

A conveyance for a house in Albemarle Road carried the following stipulation: 'No part of the land or any building erected, or to be erected thereon shall at any time be used for the purpose of the business or occupation of a Schoolmaster, Schoolmistress, Boarding Housekeeper, Auctioneer, or Estate Agent or any art or Mystery or of any trade business or manufacture whatsoever nor shall any notice or inscription board plate or placard relating to the same or any of them to be placed in or upon or about the premises and no building erected or to be erected as aforesaid shall at any time be used for any other purpose than that of a private residence'. It is no wonder that the Cator Estate was at one time considered to be the Stock Broker Belt of South London. The Cators were always quick to sense a business opportunity and soon abandoned their objections to schools when it became obvious that private education was a profitable growth industry in Beckenham and did not conflict with its high-class image.

At first the houses were not numbered but were named instead. This must have become a nightmare for the postman especially as the names were often changed when there was a new owner. One house in Albemarle Road was called 'Rolandseck' in a document dated 1894. Later it changed to 'Exford' but by 1901 it had become 'Heatherdene'. It was finally numbered No. 83. The property had been leasehold but the freehold was bought in 1963 when it changed hands once more.

In the next twenty to thirty years, however, a completely new Victorian town was to rise on what had hitherto been fields and gardens, and the centre of the town was to move to the vicinity of the station. This and later developments are reflected in the rapid growth in population, something which was to continue, apart from the war years, almost to the present time.

We are fortunate that the Ordnance Survey made a detailed large-scale study of the area in 1861. It is not only convenient but also quite legitimate to take 1857, the date of the opening of the station, as the starting point for the transformation of Beckenham from a village into a town.

Gloucester Terrace, a row of 13 houses behind the National School, had a well to provide the water supply. It was in one of these houses that the Cator Estates had their office until they later moved to a gatehouse of Beckenham Place. The

Year	Population	Inhabited Dwellings	Uninhabited Dwellings	Dwgs under construction
1801	955	159	-	-
1811	1,093	164	-	-
1821	1,180	196	-	-
1831	1,288	238	-	-
1841	1,608	285	-	-
1851	1,688	307	13	2
1861	2,124	362	10	7
1871	6,090	976	123	66
1881	13,045	1,995	175	79
1891	20,707	3,451	183	55
1901	26,331	4,701	308	166
1911	31,692	6,227	612	53
1921	33,345	6,925	267	158
1931	43,832	10,308	311	-
1941	51,000*	16,431	518#	-
1951	54,116	19,250*	348#	-
1961	56,139	20,000*	-	-

Notes: the figures for 1801 to 1931 refer to Beckenham Parish, Local Board Area and U.D.C. Area; for 1941 to 1961 they refer to the Borough of Beckenham excluding West Wickham. * - estimates. # - including West Wickham.

Sources: Census returns, Council Minutes & Housing Surveys.

18 The table above shows the population of Beckenham and was taken from an unpublished book entitled 'The Railways of Beckenham' by Andrew Hajducki. It illustrates the rapid growth of the town once the station opened.

early provision of these working-class houses illustrates that Peter Cator was well aware of the need to provide a variety of housing on his estate.

Shortlands was the other part of the parish which was developed at the same time and in a similar manner to the Cator Estates. Here the dominant landowner was W.A. Wilkinson who lived at Shortlands House from 1848 until his death in 1865. The name Shortlands may be derived from the medieval description of the size of strips of land which had been divided into cornfields or ploughed pasturage.

19   The *Station Hotel*, *c*.1905. The earliest detailed ordnance survey in 1861 shows building well under way on the Cator Estate and this hotel surrounded by orchards and gardens standing roughly where Beckenham Green is now. The hounds last met there in 1905.

Until the arrival of the railway in 1858 Shortlands, which lies mainly in the Ravensbourne valley, was known as 'a gentleman's seat, with picturesque surroundings, a farmstead and a few neat cottages'. A little later *The Bromley Record* described the large Victorian detached houses set amongst mature trees as transforming the estate into a fashionable neighbourhood. The houses in Tootswood Road and Durham Avenue were built around 1890 and further developments took place after the 1914-1918 war.

The pattern of roads was decided at a fairly early stage and usually adhered to. The 1864 Cator Estate plan which forms the inner cover of this book demonstrates this well. Mote Road was renamed The Avenue, presumably when Foxgrove Farm was demolished and the remains of the moat were filled in. The same situation applied on the Wilkinson development at Shortlands, where the roads were laid out and a church was built at a very early stage.

Whilst the Cator and Wilkinson Estates were being developed, equally rapid construction was going on in the town itself on land owned by the Cators, the Hoares at Kelsey, the Lea Wilsons of Village Place and by the Church. Rectory Road was constructed in the very early 1870s. Leases for the properties on Lea Wilson land in Lea Road, Burnhill Road and Stanmore Terrace also date from 1873 and that of Thornton's Corner a year later.

By the beginning of the 1880s the new centre of Beckenham next to the parish church was fully developed. This area was almost totally destroyed during the Second World War and the little Church Road was to disappear completely.

20   Beckenham Grove, *c.*1915. Many of the large houses in the Beckenham and Shortlands areas were used to billet soldiers during the First World War.

21   Ravensbourne Avenue, *c.*1900. The road through Summerhouse Hill Wood was never constructed as planned being replaced by Downs Hill, Crab Hill and Ravensbourne Avenue as a consequence of the Catford Loop Line development in the early 1890s.

22   The Avenue, *c.*1900. A wide, straight, tree-lined road running from Beckenham Junction through towards Shortlands, typical of the Cator Estate.

23   Shortlands Estate advertising map, *c.*1870. Most of the properties and roads illustrated can be identified today. Note, however, that the water works has been left out and the route to Beckenham made to look like a Scottish glen, presumably to improve the sales appeal!

24 Burrell Row. It is probable that the distinctive terraced properties of Burrell Row and Manor View belong to the early 1870s, providing much needed accommodation for the rapidly growing population of workers in the new shops and service trades.

In 1866 the Duke of Westminster sold Porcupine Field in Beckenham, close to Penge East station, on very favourable terms to the 'Metropolitan Association for Improving the Dwellings of the Industrious Classes'. On this land the charity erected its only country estate and named it 'Alexandra' after the Princess of Wales. The four roads were named Albert, Edward, Victor, and Princess (later changed to Princes).

The Birkbeck Estate was begun in the 1870s when land was bought by the Birkbeck Freehold Land Society. It was not fully developed until just before the First World War when Allen Road was built. The Churchfields Road area had belonged to the Beckenham Parish Church Council. This is why Seward and Clement Roads are the only two roads having direct links between Churchfields and Blandford Roads as they were built on the only plot of land owned by the Birkbeck Estate. It also accounts for the reason why Sultan Street and Blandford Avenue are culs-de-sac and Kimberley Road is a crescent.

25 The High Street, *c.*1903. Note the Royal Coat of Arms over number 3, Haggers the butchers.

26 The High Street end of Albemarle Road in 1905 was very busy, having shops and the main post office.

27 Albert Road, seen here *c.*1910, was unusual as the houses were semi-detached and each had a garden at a time when most Victorian working-class houses were terraces or tenements.

If the Cator and Wilkinson Estates were to provide the earliest high-class housing developments in Beckenham, they were to be followed later by one even more ambitious. In 1908 the firm of H. & G. Taylor purchased the bulk of the Langley Estate, including the mansion, from the trustees of the Goodhart Estate. The estate they planned was to be self contained with its own shopping centre, post office, community hall, tennis courts and golf course, but significantly no church.

The cost of these magnificent homes seems almost unbelievable today. In an example quoted in the sales brochure, a house costing £850 is purchased by paying £200 down, borrowing the remainder from an Assurance Co. and repaying this over 20 years in half-yearly instalments totalling £56 2s. 4d. per annum. Whitecroft Way was one of the first roads on the new estate. It was named after Richard de Wytecroft who lived in the 13th century and was connected with Langley. There

28   Birkbeck Road, *c.*1909. There was a footbridge across the railway between the two parts of the Birkbeck Estate and before the Second World War this was closed one day a year to indicate it was railway property and not a public right of way.

had been a road there for some centuries running from Langley to Foxgrove. One of the first houses to be erected in Whitecroft Way won an award at the 1912 Ideal Homes Exhibition.

Apart from laying out the roads, many of which were named after historic persons connected with the estate on the recommendation of Robert Borrowman, the first development was the golf club. A club house had been built onto the old mansion, which had required substantial renovation after lying empty since 1903 when it was vacated by the Goodharts. Sadly, both were destroyed by fire in 1913 and replaced with the present club house. The club was opened by its newly elected President, Mr H.W. Forster, M.P. on 28 May 1910. Tennis followed soon after and nine courts had been laid down by 1911.

29 Wickham Way, *c.*1925. The houses were all to be architecturally designed in a variety of sizes and styles with no two exactly alike. Each was to have a substantial garden and be approached from tree and shrub lined roads, partially to conceal them from the gaze of casual passers-by. Even the lamp posts were specially designed for the estate.

30 Coldman House, *c.*1920. Unlike the Victorian and Edwardian houses of the Cator and Wilkinson estates, Taylor's houses looked surprisingly modern and, apart from the size of the gardens, would not look out of place on a present-day up-market development. Noticeable too for the period is the lack of staff accommodation and the provision of a garage.

31 Elmers End shops, *c.*1907. This parade of shops is between Langley Road and Goddard Road. The *William IV* public house can be seen at the end of the road on the left.

32 *Above*. Langley Road, Elmers End, *c*.1910. Houses did not extend the full length of Goddard Road until a few council houses were built at the top end in the 1920s.

33 *Left*. Upper Elmers End Road, *c*.1925. With the building of the council estate, Elmers End changed more than most of the parish.

34   Eden Way was built in 1936 almost on the boundary of the Borough.

Unlike the sporting facilities, the other planned amenities were never provided. This is a pity, for the shopping centre, planned for what is now the junction of Styles and Whitecroft Way, was a truly remarkable proposal for the day. It was to consist of a circle of shops with flats over the top and a covered winter garden with bandstand, palms and statuary in the centre. The development attracted a lot of attention and seems to have made steady progress, though whether the plans for a motor bus service—which it was claimed would meet the principal trains at Beckenham Junction—was ever carried out is not certain. The outbreak of war stopped the building completely. Much of the post-war development was carried out by others and at a somewhat lower standard.

The Taylors seem to have had a flair for publicity and, when in 1929 they opened a garage at Looking Glass Corner at the entrance to the estate, it was built in Eastern style and ever since it has been known as the Chinese Garage.

There was a reference to Elmers End in an indenture dated 1682 relating to 'house, buildings, grounds and land known as "Eastfield" situated at Elmers End, occupied by Stephen Randell and Thomas Fanster'. Another early reference was

35 Elmers End, seen here early in the 20th century, was virtually all farm land and woods, a very rural part of Beckenham. It remained largely undeveloped until after the First World War.

36 An early view of the Davies Estate. The Drive was originally to be called 'Wilson Avenue' but the proposal was overruled by the Council.

in 1775 when mention was made of the great want for small houses for the 'industrious shepherds and labourers of the Parish'. It was decided to ask John Cator, the Lord of the Manor, to build 12 houses—four of which were those put up near to the *William IV* at Elmers End Green and another four near the *Rising Sun*. These latter ones were demolished in 1962 to make way for new council flats.

It was not until much later that Elmers End was really developed. Besides the cottages at the *William IV* there was a parade of shops on the other side of Croydon Road, with a few quite large houses in Langley Road. The district came into its own with the building between 1920 and 1930 of the council estate in Goddard and Adams Roads and Shirley Crescent to provide accommodation for local workers, some at the nearby factories of Twinlock and Muirheads. At the same time housing developments were started in the Eden Park area. By the early 1930s most of the available land had been covered with the exception of the playing fields in Stanhope Grove, Balmoral Avenue, and the back of Marian Vian School.

At the end of the 1914-18 war there was still a lot of open country in the parish and working farms could be found within walking distance of the High Street. Even the centre of the town was taken up by gardens and meadows belonging either to the Lea-Wilsons or the Church. By 1939 most of this land had been built on and the town had become—in fact, if not in name—part of London. Village Place was demolished and its grounds together with those of the Rectory replaced by the Davis Estate of small terrace houses selling for £950 and the new roads of The Drive, Church Avenue and The Crescent.

This rapid development of the southern part and centre of the town at a much higher density than the older Cator, Wilkinson and Taylor Estates resulted in a marked move of the centre of the commercial town back to its original position along the lower High Street. This was assisted by the Council who had compulsorily purchased land along almost its entire length so that it could be widened. It incidentally resulted in the replacement of the old shops by more modern properties which were taken up by firms such as Montague Burton, W.H. Smith, Boot's and Woolworth's.

Three

Beckenham Town

Administration and Services

Until 1872 the only authority dealing with local affairs within the parish was the vestry, a committee of local landowners and gentry chaired by the Rector. The records of Beckenham vestry have survived from 1774 as have a few isolated ones dating back to the 1680s. It was a versatile body which dealt with both public and church matters, many of which are still relevant today. In 1778 we read of it conducting a survey on the willingness of the inhabitants to be inoculated against smallpox at the parish expense. A few years later Sunday observance was a hot subject. The vestry decided that no shop should sell any goods after ten in the morning nor should any individual shave or dress their hair after the same hour. Anyone found offending was liable to be placed in the 'Cage' and left to ponder the inscription over the door: 'Live and Repent'.

The vestry in 1869 passed a resolution that 'as it was difficult to keep the old and thickly filled churchyard in order by hand the Churchwardens at St George's church should be authorised to admit sheep for the purpose'.

The construction of the London to Croydon canal which passed through the north-west corner of the parish and its replacement in 1839 by a railway led to an influx of navvies into the area. It was, however, the construction of the Crystal Palace in 1852-4, a considerable part of the grounds of which was in Beckenham, that had the most far-reaching effect. At that time scant regard was paid to parish or even county boundaries for the financial and planning implications were minimal.

37 Disorderly and inebriated persons would be put in the Cage until they sobered up. It was at the bottom of Church Hill and was removed in November 1856.

31

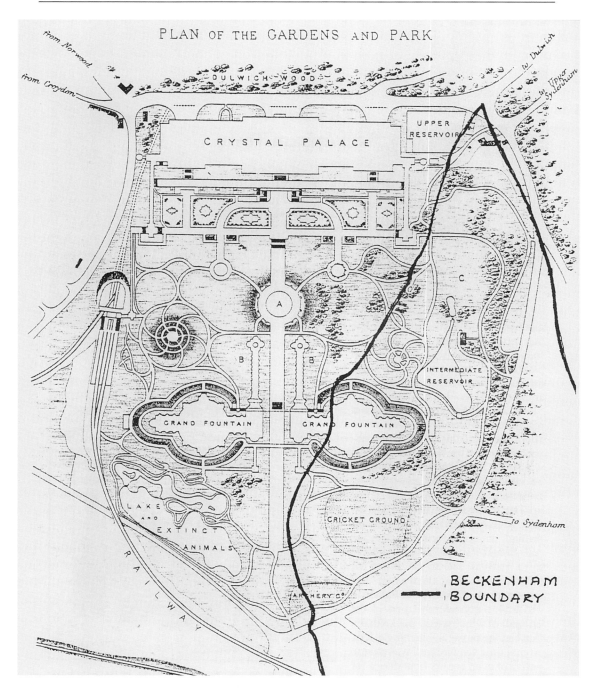

38 The Crystal Palace grounds straddled the Kent-Surrey boundary and involved no fewer than the three parishes of Battersea, Dulwich and Beckenham. During construction, the streets of the once peaceful village resounded to the boots of two hundred navvies who lodged in Beckenham and walked, two miles each way, to and from their work.

39 The old fire and police stations. When No. 7 Kelsey Square was being re-decorated in 1961, a painted panel was discovered under the layers of wallpaper in the passageway, giving details of the Offices and Officers of the Board.

Once completed, the enormous glasshouse, ablaze with light in the evenings and replete with every modern development, was visible from almost every part of the parish, a constant reminder of the technical changes taking place in the world outside. As a result of the opening of the palace, land in the north-west part of the parish became much in demand for building large houses with mains water provided by the Lambeth Water Co. and gas by the Crystal Palace and District Co. at Bell Green, Sydenham, luxuries which soon became available in the rest of the parish.

The rapid development in housing, particularly in the part of the parish nearest to the Crystal Palace, compelled the vestry to introduce a measure of control over the activities of its residents and the disposal of their waste. A sanitary sub-committee had already been set up in 1848 to remove nuisances such as ill-sited pig-sties. Ten years later this became a Nuisances Removal Committee with increased powers granted under an 1855 Act of Parliament.

The 1872 Public Health Act divided the country into Urban and Rural Sanitary Districts whose authorities took over most of the duties formerly exercised by the parish vestry. Beckenham found itself in the Bromley Rural Sanitary District with its affairs administered by a Parochial Sub-Committee. This was an affront to many of the inhabitants of the rapidly growing township and in 1878 it was authorised to elect a Local Board, able to appoint officers and decide its own affairs independently of Bromley. This remained the case until 1894 when increased urbanisation led Kent County Council to replace the Board with an Urban District Council.

40   Bromley Road with Bank, Public Hall and Old Council Hall, *c.*1909. Much of the cost of the Old Manor House was recouped by selling off parts of the garden to the London & County Bank (now part of the National Westminster Bank) and to the Metropolitan Police.

The Beckenham Local Board set up office above the fire station building, which had been provided for that purpose by Peter Hoare of Kelsey, and later converted two of the adjacent dwelling houses in Kelsey Square into additional accommodation. This extra space was soon totally inadequate so in 1882 the opportunity was taken to purchase the old Manor House and the immediately adjacent garden and outhouses for £5,075 including fittings. The older part of the Manor House was demolished and its site sold to a Public Hall Company set up for the purpose. The remaining building required only little adaptation. The stables were extended to house the fire brigade with accomodation for seven horses and a loft above for hay and fodder. A new front was added in 1884/5 to tone in with the adjoining new bank premises and, sadly, this is the only part of the building to survive until the present day.

The town continued to grow rapidly as did the services required to be provided by the Council. The Education Office moved to 14, Bromley Road; the Public Health Office to the building on the corner of Burnhill Road and the High Street; the Surveyor's Department to a shop on Church Hill, while the Electricity Show-rooms, then part of the Council's administration, were on the corner of Manor Road and Church Hill.

In 1926 the Council purchased the old rectory and much of its garden for the construction of a town hall large enough to accommodate all the Council departments for the foreseeable future. A successful application for approval and grant aid as an unemployment relief scheme enabled opposition on the grounds of excessive debt to be overcome.

41 Opening of the new Town Hall. On 20 October 1932 the building was declared open by HRH Prince George, Duke of Kent. The school children who lined the route managed to cheer loudly in spite of the rain.

42 The Town Hall, *c.*1935. Beckenham Council was able to organise its affairs much more efficiently once all departments were housed in one central building.

Whilst awaiting the construction of its new town hall in 1931 the Council acquired a grant of arms. The green shield symbolises the town's rural setting emphasised by two flowering horse chestnut trees. The wavy lines symbolise the Beck under which is the white horse of Kent. In September 1935 the town was granted Municipal Borough status and the Lord Mayor of London arrived in his state coach to present the Charter of Incorporation to the Mayor and Council. To commemorate this occasion two supporters in 16th-century costume were added to the crest. The motto, 'non nobis solum', translates as 'not for ourselves alone'.

Beckenham's pride was to be short-lived. Between the wars every piece of open ground not dedicated as parkland was built up and by 1939 housing estates had obscured the boundaries between the separate communities which had formerly made up the area. Urban facilities were now more appropriate than those designed for rural commmunities and it was for this reason that in 1934 West Wickham had become part of Beckenham Urban District. In 1965 the final blow fell—the town was transferred from the County of Kent to Greater London. Worse still, administration became centred in Bromley and Beckenham became part of the London Borough of Bromley. The Council buildings in which the town had taken so much pride gradually became redundant and were demolished, the old Council Hall in 1990 and the Town Hall itself in 1992.

During its brief thirty years of existence as an independent borough Beckenham granted its freedom to only five people: Alderman James Crease and Sir Josiah Stamp in 1936, the Right Hon Winston Churchill in 1946, Dr James Bennett and Alderman W.J. Sampson in 1955. Sir Josiah Stamp, Lord Stamp of Shortlands, was President and Chairman of the LMS Railway as well as being the Charter Mayor of Beckenham. He, together with his family, were tragically killed in their home in Shortlands during an air raid. In 1992 an Intercity class 90 electric locomotive was named 'Lord Stamp' in his honour.

So far we have concentrated on the development of local government in the town but services also grew in size and complexity and, just like administration, were gradually taken out of local hands.

Probably the first undertaking to be run by the local authority, apart from road maintenance, was the workhouse and it was also the first to pass into the hands of a larger authority, in this case the Bromley Union, in 1836. It is not known when the workhouse opened but it was sited on the Bromley Road well away from the village itself. Its spartan conditions were described in some detail in Borrowman's *Beckenham, Past and Present*. There were 14 beds in all, so that, on occasions when the house had over 24 inmates, it must have been very overcrowded. Lights were not allowed except in the hall, which was lit with three candlesticks. The supply of towels for the whole establishment never exceeded eight, and ablutions were probably made under the pump in the yard. The supply of sheets for the 14 beds never exceeded 29, and there was only one pillow case! According to the inventories there was only one flannel gown, used no doubt for the invalids. The comforts were not very attractive and it was not uncommon for the inmates to run away. When caught they were put in the lock-up which was scantily furnished with a chaff bed and a blanket.

43   Fire practice at Foxgrove Farm, *c*.1875. Until 1886 Charles Purvis, the tenant of Foxgrove Farm, was the Hon. Superintendent and it was at the farm that the brigade did much of its practice.

The police was the first service to become London-based. With the growth of population and crime, the village constable appointed by the vestry had become quite inappropriate. Alderman Wilson who lived in Village Place applied in 1833 for Beckenham to come under the jurisdiction of the Metropolitan Police and, when six years later he became Lord Mayor of London, his request was granted. A cottage next to the *Three Tuns* public house became the police station manned by a sergeant and seven constables. By 1865 this had become two sergeants and 10 constables under the supervision of a mounted inspector based at Lewisham. The present police station on Church Hill was built on part of the Old Manor House garden purchased from the Local Board and was opened by Squire Lea Wilson on 1 June 1885. The old police station was demolished in 1936 to provide access for parking behind the *Three Tuns*.

The local gentry were concerned not only about crime but also the dangers of fire. Sir Francis Tress Barry of Clock House organised a volunteer brigade for which Peter Hoare adapted one of the buildings at the entrance to the Kelsey Estate to house the 'engine'. The brigade passed into the control of the Local Board and moved to a new station adapted from the Old Manor House stables in 1882. The original fire station remains to this day, its interior much altered and now occupied by a hairdresser. Fires must have burnt fairly slowly in those days for not only had the local turncock to be roused to turn on the water, horses had also to be acquired for harnessing to the engine. At that time any passing vehicle could be stopped and its horse used for the fire engine. In July 1885 there was a fire in Southend Lane and the engine couldn't go because the horse was ill! The gallant firemen proceeded to the scene by cab. Apparently no-one thought to put the cab horse to the fire engine!

The large area covered by the parish and the slow speed of the appliances on the rough unmade roads necessitated sub-depots to cover areas such as Birkbeck, Lawrie Park and Shortlands. For example, in 1890 a hose reel shed was erected in Valley Road next to the parish room and replaced in 1902 by a purpose-built engine house with accommodation in Station Road. This sub-station closed in 1913 when the brigade acquired its second motor fire engine and was later demolished. The Birkbeck station was in Avenue Road and a third one in Alexandra Recreation Ground.

The Bromley Road fire station was extended and adapted over the years. It housed at one time or another a social club, a dentist, and the Saunders and Abbott motor dealers. In 1929 the Council built houses for the firemen at the rear of the station and later, after the incorporation of West Wickham, a modern station was opened in Glebe Way. The war resulted in the demise of small local brigades with

their limited resources and varying, often incompatible, equipment. All brigades were nationalised from 1941 to 1948 and, after this, responsibility for firefighting in Beckenham passed first to Kent County Council and then, after the 1965 local government reorganisation, to the London Fire Brigade. As a result the West Wickham Fire station was closed and the Bromley Road station replaced by a combined fire and ambulance station in Beckenham Road, which opened in 1986.

Even by the middle of the 19th century services in Beckenham were much simpler than today. Water was obtained from wells and pumps and the waste from primitive privies ran into cess pools often sited in close proximity to the water supply. None of the village pumps have survived; that at the corner of Kelsey Square is a spout installed by the Lambeth Water Company to service the fire brigade horses. One of the pumps stood in the middle of the road at the bottom

of Church Hill. The first public sewer was constructed in 1860, and Borrowman recalls that a few years later Dr Stilwell called the attention of the vestry to the impure water supply which existed in the village. The Shortlands pumping station came into use in the 1860s.

The building of the Crystal Palace, partly in the parish, meant that not only was the Beckenham parish vestry's permission required to supply gas and water to the venture but there was a strong and growing commercial incentive to do so. Thames water was supplied by the Lambeth Water Company from a reservoir near the Palace and many were the complaints about its quality and continuity until 1903 when all the private water companies in the London area were taken over by the newly constituted Metropolitan Water Board. Lambeth's water did not reach as far as Wilkinson's Shortlands estate; this was pumped from a well sunk in a meadow near the railway by the North Kent Water Co.

44 Beckenham's 'First Aid Tri-Car' was purchased in 1908 at a cost of £122. It was designed for two firemen with basic equipment to rush to a blaze to do what they could whilst the main engine was 'horsed up' and could come galloping to the scene!

45   Beckenham Cottage Hospital , *c.*1911. The hospital opened in 1872 through the generosity of Peter Hoare of Kelsey Manor who provided both the land and building for a four-bed hospital at a nominal rent.

On 2 September 1854, the vestry gave the Crystal Palace & District Gas Co. permission to introduce gas into the parish at their expense and some time later three street lamps were erected, one at the junction of Penge (now Beckenham) and Croydon Roads, one in the vicinity of the Cage and Pound, and one near the rectory gate. There was no street lighting prior to this and once the sun went down the only light in even the grandest of homes came from candles or oil lamps. In 1864 street lighting was extended to include the whole length of the road from Penge to Beckenham Junction. The *George Inn* was one of the first buildings in Beckenham to be lit by gas.

Beckenham Cottage Hospital is yet another example of local initiative and generosity providing a service which in its time was a source of great local pride only to decline later into the relative obscurity of a large regional authority. Patients were charged sixpence a day and the building also housed public baths and wash houses. Peter Hoare's death in 1877 resulted in a crisis as his estate demanded a commercial rent. The value of the facility was so appreciated that donations not only enabled this rent to be paid but the freehold to be purchased in 1887. A year later, a four-room extension named after Squire Lea Wilson was added. An operating theatre was built, followed only two years later by a children's ward and an almost doubling of the hospital's capacity to 31 beds. X-ray facilities were provided by Messrs Muirhead of Elmers End in 1902. In 1921 an additional ward was opened to commemorate Beckenham's war dead.

The hospital passed into the hands of the state in 1948 but expansion still continued almost to the present time when uncertainty as to its future role has cast a cloud over the scene. Beckenham's hospital facilities were not confined to the Cottage Hospital. Maternity services were provided at a house in Croydon Road from 1919 until 1939 when a purpose-built maternity hospital opened in Stone Park Avenue. This was closed in 1986 and the site sold to Morden College. In 1924 the world renowned Bethlem Hospital purchased Monks Orchard estate on the Beckenham border and was opened on its new site by H.M. Queen Mary.

46 Stone Park Maternity Hospital. This replaced the Beckenham and Penge Maternity Home in 1939 and closed in 1986. The site is now a sheltered housing complex owned by Morden College.

47 The Anthony Rawlins almshouses before they were modernised in the 1880s.

48 This power station, situated off Arthur Road, was opened by the Council in 1900. It used water from the nearby stream for cooling and domestic rubbish as part of its fuel.

Beckenham has had three almshouses since 1694 when Anthony Rawlins left a bequest of £50 so that these might be built. They were modernised in the 1880s and are still in use at the side of the parish church.

The presence of the Crystal Palace, a major electrical factory (Muirheads), and a large wealthy population resulted in Beckenham Council having a very forward-thinking attitude to the production and use of electricity in the parish. The Local Board first applied for an Electric Lighting Order for the parish in 1882 but this was only to thwart an application by a private company and was not pursued. The Board did nothing until 10 years later when the Crystal Palace and District Electric Lighting Supply Company, based just outside the parish in Sydenham, obtained an Order which included the Lawrie Park part of Beckenham. It must be remembered that at this time even gas lighting was a luxury which only the well-off could afford. Beckenham got its own order in 1893 and the generating station, situated at the depot in Churchfields Road, opened on 22 November 1900, consuming the town's refuse as part of its fuel, one of the first examples of practical re-cycling.

An electricity showroom was opened on the corner of Manor Road in 1910 where it remained until in 1932 it moved into magnificent purpose built premises, an integral part of the new Town Hall. Beckenham lost control of the undertaking on nationalisation in 1948 although long before this supplies had been taken from the national grid and local generation abandoned. The showroom was closed soon after the London Electricity Board was privatised and in 1992 it was demolished to make way for a Marks & Spencer food store.

The first large-scale practical use of electricity was for communication. The electric telegraph came to Beckenham with the railways but passed to the control of the Post Office in 1869 when it was gradually made available at all major post offices. The telephone appeared surprisingly early. Beckenham was initially served from the National Telephone Company's exchange in Bromley which opened sometime before 1890 and was renamed Ravensbourne in 1924 to avoid confusion with

Croydon when automatic dialling was introduced. Beckenham got its own exchange, which is still in use, in July 1928.

Whilst Beckenham was a tiny village the churchyard at the parish church had been adequate, but as the population increased it became obvious that further ground would be needed. The extension of the churchyard in 1868 only helped for a very short time and in 1876 the Elmers End cemetery opened. Beckenham churchyard was closed for burials in 1890 except for families with existing rights, some of which still apply, e.g. Rob Copeland.

The Crystal Palace and District Cemetery Co. Ltd, now called Birkbeck Securities Ltd, traces its origins back to the London and Suburban Land and Building Society set up in 1852 as one of the associations whose aims were to acquire land and thus obtain a vote under the 1832 Reform Act. It became a Limited Company in 1863 and five years later purchased 41 acres at Elmers End from William Cator for £12,000. In 1870 it was decided that use of the site for a cemetery would be a good investment and outline approval from the Secretary of State was obtained. In order to develop the site and meet the Government and religious requirements, a new company was formed in 1873. It is believed that this is the oldest commercial cemetery company in the country. The last war brought to an end nearly seventy years of increasing trade and prosperity so in the 1950s the Company diversified into cremations. One of the original chapels was converted into a crematorium in 1956 and its capacity doubled in 1960. Ten years later the company name was changed to Beckenham Crematorium Ltd, and in 1997 it was acquired by the American firm, Service Company International. The cemetery services a wide area, not only Beckenham. It contains the graves of a number of distinguished people including Thomas Crapper the famous Victorian plumber, W.G. Grace, the cricketer, Frederick Wolseley, the car manufacturer, and William Walker the diver who saved Winchester Cathedral.

49 Elmers End Cemetery poster can still be seen in the cemetery office and clearly depicts the rural nature of the area.

50   The London & Provincial Bank on the corner of Rectory Road, *c.*1910. This bank, now part of
Barclays, opened in Beckenham in 1874 and operated from this site, formerly part of the rectory
garden, for 114 years until 1988, when it moved to modern premises on the corner of Beckenham
Road. The old building is now a Thai restaurant.

Both the London and Provincial and the London and Counties Banks opened
branches in Beckenham in 1874, the former in a chemist's shop run by the local
postmaster. Within ten years the two rivals had moved into purpose-built premises,
the former now part of Barclays, on the corner of Rectory Road where it operated
for 108 years, and the latter, now part of National Westminster, on the corner of
Bromley Road where it remains to the present day. In 1898 the Midland (now
HSBC) opened on the corner of Mackenzie Road where it stayed until 1962 when
it moved to Penge. It was 1925 before the Midland was represented in central
Beckenham, followed three years later by Lloyds.

The development of the postal service is yet another indicator of the quick-
ening pulse of activity in an area. Beckenham's first pillar box was in Park Road
but cannot be the present one as this is of 1887-1904 vintage. By 1866, the
postmaster was listed as Richard East, Beckenham Village. Three years later
Thomas Sweeting Day, the chemist near Beckenham Junction, had become the
postmaster. Beckenham was now a post town addressed as Beckenham, Kent and
not Beckenham S.E. as previously. By the late 1870s the post office had moved
round the corner to Mrs Peverill's stationery shop. In later years this became a
crown post office. In 1897 a purpose-built office was opened in Albemarle Road
on the site now occupied by St George's Parish Church Hall. It remained there
until 1939 when the present main post office took over. Beckenham by then had

51 Roger's grocers shop and Post Office in the High Street, 1869. At the introduction of uniform penny postage in 1840 Beckenham's only post office was here. Letters arrived and departed by mailcart to and from London four times a day.

52 Beckenham's main Post Office in 1897 was decorated for the Queen's Diamond Jubilee just before it moved to the new building further up Albemarle Road.

53 The new Post Office and Sorting Office in 1897. The purpose-built office is seen here with its builders. When the Post Office closed in 1939 the building was used for a succession of other businesses.

five sub-offices and nine pillar boxes. The sub-offices are listed as High Street, Bromley Road, Avenue Road Birkbeck, Kent House, and Elmers End. In 2001 the delivery office, now a separate organisation from the counters operation, moved to purpose-built industrial premises at Elmers End.

In the *Beckenham Journal Jubilee Edition* of 1936 a Mrs Town, then 89 years of age, relates a story concerning the mail cart at a time when, according to her, there was no post office in the place; the mail was left at the police station. As according to Pigot there was a post office in 1835 and the police station did not appear until 1839, this cannot be strictly true. The story was that the driver had frozen to death in his cart and the horse pulled up outside and waited until the police came out to investigate. A Mr Glover, who was then 84, states that in his youth there were, he fancies, only about three postmen (and about three policemen, which we know to be wrong); the mails were sent to and from Bromley by road. The driver of the mail cart announced his arrival at the post office by sounding his horn. He pins down the approximate date by describing the station as a terminus with a turntable.

Four

Transport

Rail, Public and Private Road Transport and Associated Trades

Improvements in transport have had more influence on the development of Beckenham than any other factor. The town's initial combination of nearness to London and remoteness from a main road encouraged larger estates which changed once the village had its own direct rail service.

Beckenham's first public transport was a twice-weekly coach service to London, which started in 1715 when the roads resembled what we today would regard as cart tracks—dusty in summer, rutted and almost impassable in bad weather. They were the responsibility of the local vestry, apart from the route from Lewisham to Croydon which in 1765 was under the care of the New Cross Turnpike Trust. By 1839, a coach named 'The Accommodation' was running every morning to London and returning the same day. Later, when Sydenham station on the London to Croydon Railway opened, William Legg, who lived at Elm Cottage, on the corner of what is now Village Way, started an omnibus service to meet the trains, which was later taken over by William Ovenden, the licensee of the *Three Tuns*. By 1855, just before the village got its own station, an omnibus was running four times daily, starting from the *White Hart* in Bromley.

The London to Croydon Railway replaced the canal of the same name which had opened in 1809 and closed in 1836. Both the canal and the railway passed through the north-west corner of Beckenham parish affording a modest revenue to the vestry which assessed the latter at £9 in 1839. In 1854 a branch line was built, passing through the parish, to serve the newly opened Crystal Palace. By this time work was well under way by the West London & Crystal Palace Railway to construct a branch from London Bridge to Beckenham via New Cross and Catford. Beckenham station opened in January 1857, making it older than most of the present London termini. Within a year a single-line extension had been built to Shortlands to serve Bromley, and an alternative route constructed to London via Crystal Palace. Beckenham station was renamed Beckenham Junction and its turntable was removed.

In 1863, what had become the London, Chatham & Dover Railway opened a more direct line to London through a tunnel under Sydenham Hill and with a station called Penge East which, despite its name, was in Beckenham. The following year the South Eastern Railway, which had by now absorbed the Mid-Kent Company, started a line to the east side of Croydon with stations at New Beckenham and

Elmers End. Thus in seven years the bulk of the complex rail system which now serves all parts of the parish had been created. The only later additions were the Hayes branch, opened in 1882, and the Shortlands to Nunhead railway 10 years later. Rapid development in the north of the parish resulted in the subsequent opening of three more stations—Kent House station in 1884, Clock House station in 1890, and finally Birkbeck, which did not open until March 1930. Many of the early stations were built in what was then open country in anticipation of rapid building development in the vicinity, but this did not always take place. The first New Beckenham station closed after two years when it was found that there was insufficient traffic to justify separate services to Addiscombe and Beckenham. This division is the reason for the wide spacing of the platforms. Originally there was a third track to enable engines to run round the train when the Beckenham and Addiscombe portions were separated. Lower Sydenham station on the same line was once outside the parish and moved to its present position in 1906. The lines all crossed the Cator's Beckenham Estate and were constructed with the active involvement of the Cators and other big landowners who provided land and access on very favourable terms. The owners were concerned that provision of this access did not reduce the value and amenity of their estates and placed restrictions on the operating companies, particularly as regards manure trains lingering too long and trains stopping at stations on the estate during divine service on Sundays.

At first the railways prospered, as they provided the best means of travel for the rapidly growing population of businessmen who needed to reach their offices in the City each day. Beckenham trains, it was said, were famous for having passengers standing in the first class whilst the second- and third-class compartments were nearly empty! Nevertheless the subjects of the many letters of complaint which filled the newspapers of the day seem very similar to the ones we read today. The trains did improve when the system was electrified in 1925 soon after the formation of the Southern Railway.

55 Beckenham Junction, *c*.1912. A typical scene in the days of steam. Milk churns from the local farms can be seen awaiting despatch.

56 New Beckenham Station in 1993. A level crossing, which was situated where the pedestrian underpass is now, was closed in 1900 when Bridge Road was opened and the station itself was rebuilt in stages, finishing in 1904.

57 Forecourt at Shortlands' Station, *c*.1914. A station-master's house occupied what is now the present car park site.

58 Despite its name, Penge East Station is in Beckenham but ironically Beckenham Hill Station is in Lewisham. The date of this picture is *c*.1905.

59 These commuters stroll home from Kent House Station in the evening, although in the morning they had run to catch their trains.

60 Even today Ravensbourne Station, seen here *c*.1900, is approached from an unmade section of a Cator Estate road and still has a very rural look about it.

61 'The Beckenham Horse Bus' early in the 20th century. The driver collected the fares through a hole in the roof and also controlled access by using his foot to operate the catch on the door.

The first threat to the trains came from the electric trams which very nearly reached Beckenham. In 1902 an attempt to get a Bill through Parliament authorising a line from Penge to Thornton's Corner, and straightening up the High Street in the process, met violent opposition from the residents who felt it would lower the tone of the place. In 1905 the Council, taking the view that trams were inevitable, succeeded in getting its own tramway Bill through Parliament, but the project foundered as terms could not be agreed with the contractors. So from 1906 until 1936 trams ran through Penge, powered by electricity supplied by Beckenham, but stopping at Thicket Road, near the Beckenham boundary. In May 2000 trams finally came to Beckenham with the opening of Tramlink, providing a fast and frequent service from Beckenham Junction to Croydon and from Elmers End to Wimbledon. This involved the sacrifice of the little-used Elmers End to Addiscombe branch line after 136 years and the resurrection of the short-lived halt at Beckenham Road.

From about 1895 until January 1914 the route which the trams would have taken was served by Tilling's Shortlands to Penge horse bus, popularly known as 'Noah's Ark' . Thomas Tilling, who had started his business in 1847 with one horse, dominated the South London transport scene at this time. His company had two depots in Beckenham, one at the side of the *Oakhill Tavern* and another beside the *Station Hotel* in the High Street.

In Victorian times people of consequence in Beckenham would own horses and in most cases employed a coachman as well. So numerous were these employees in the town that they could raise a cricket team to play the gardeners. At this time people thought nothing of walking several miles and with no less than 12 railway stations within the parish the lack of a good public bus system was not the disadvantage it would be today.

In 1896 it became legal for the first time to drive a vehicle weighing less than three tons on the public highway without the need to have someone walking in front to warn other road users of its approach. The obligation of this person to carry a red flag had already been removed in 1878. Tilling started to motorise his bus services in 1904 and the Shortlands to Penge route was one of the last to be converted. The last horse bus ran at 11.30 p.m. on 3 January 1914 but it was not until 1 June that the 112 motor bus service from the *White Hart*, Bromley to Thicket Road, Penge started. The following month service 113, Beckenham Junction to Park Langley, also commenced, both services using vehicles based at Catford Garage. They ceased abruptly on the outbreak of war as all the buses were requisitioned for military duties. The service was resumed as No. 109 and extended to Woolwich in the latter half of the war to provide transport for munitions workers at the Arsenal. It was suspended once the war ended and the need for munitions work ceased but, after protests, it resumed in September 1919 with a terminus at Bromley North, extended to Chislehurst six months later. The 1984 London Regional Transport Act heralded a new era with competitive tendering and the appearance of new companies and introduction of new routes. Particularly conspicuous in Beckenham is the blue and yellow livery of Metrobus, a company founded in 1963 and noted for pioneering new services.

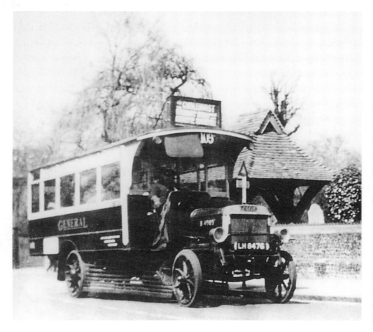

62 A service 109 bus outside the parish church in the 1920s. After the war the number and variety of bus services grew rapidly and by 1935 no fewer than 85 buses a day were passing through Beckenham High Street. In 1934 the newly formed London Passenger Transport Board did away with the old police numbering system and the 109 Penge to Bromley service, seen here, acquired its familiar 227 route number.

63 Elmers End Bus Garage in 1937. This garage received a direct hit by a VI flying bomb during the war and many of its buses were destroyed in the ensuing fire. Eighteen people lost their lives in this incident. The garage closed in 1986 but the memorial plaque was saved and can now be seen in the London Transport Museum.

There were several toll gates on the approaches to the Cator Estate until the turn of the century. The one at Kent House Farm existed until 1883 and that in Lennard Road, opposite Holy Trinity church, was removed in 1894. The nearest toll gate to Beckenham is now at Dulwich near the College and the charge for a car has recently been increased to 50p.

By the 1880s bicycles were an important and fashionable means of transport. The earliest mention of a cycle dealer in Beckenham in the surviving directories is that in 1890 of Walter Bourdon & Co. of Station Approach. There are almost certainly earlier traders for J.W. Tostevin of the Kelsey Cycle Works claimed 24 years' experience in 1903 though this may not all have been in Beckenham. By 1914 seven dealers are listed, three of whom also claimed to be motor engineers. Garages were initially extensions of existing businesses such as blacksmiths, coach builders or cycle dealers and only gradually specialised in the motor trade. For example, Mr Padbury, whose forge features prominently on many postcards, next

door to the old wood house in the High Street, was by 1914 advertising that he also
repaired, painted and upholstered motors at a depot three doors from the Public
Hall, i.e next door to the fire station. Likewise Mr Tostevin of the Kelsey Cycle
Works not only dealt in pedal cycles and repaired perambulators, mail carts and
bath chairs but also supplied motor cycles. This made sense, for not only was the
early motor business very much a cottage industry, but servicing horse-drawn traffic
remained by far the more important activity until well after the end of the First
World War.

G.W. Clarke made the 'Beckenham' cycle and advertised himself as a Cycle
and General Engineer and sole agent for Humber, Singer, Enfield and Triumph
cycles. He also sold petrol and is presumably the same man who is listed in the
1914 *Directory* as a motor engineer with premises at 1 Wickham Road, which in
1926 were occupied by Saunders & Abbott. His 1902 address was at the side of the
Conservative Club, later occupied by John Pillin, also a motor engineer.

The Siren Motor Works is listed at 59a High Street, a former builder's yard
situated between Howards Stores and the *George*. This company developed into
the Beckenham Motor Co. with extensive premises, including garaging for 50 cars,
situated further down the High Street at number 181, between Hitt's Stores and
Burrell Row. Its most famous owner was James T. Batten who lived in Cedars
Road. It was here that he built so many of his 'specials', which were constructed
for hill climbs and trials during the 1920s. Batten and his friend and colleague,
Challenor Barson, son of a Penge Congregational minister, were often to be seen
and heard driving these strange hybrids, dressed in overalls and back to front cap
and goggles. The outbreak of hostilities caused the company to be wound up in

64   Three production Batten Specials, *c*.1937. The one on the left of the picture was the last of
these cars, a coupé specially built for Lord Plunkett.

March 1940. Soon afterwards James Batten was engaged in secret development work for the army and in post-war years he worked with the Rootes Group.

Most of the early motor businesses in Beckenham are now part of the Masters Group based in Upper Elmers End Road. Its story starts with Ronald Stoneham, whose family had a long history of interest in and ownership of cars. In 1930 Ron moved from New Cross and opened a small café in Upper Elmers End Road. This did so well that in 1952 he was able to acquire his first garage, a modest affair called Vincents founded in 1930 near the *Rising Sun*. Four years later he added the Copers Cope Garage which had been founded by Roderick Selfe as the Albemarle garage soon after the end of the First World War. In 1963 he moved his head-quarters a few yards along the road to the present purpose-built showroom and workshop. In 1968 he acquired the famous Chinese Garage and in 1979 the garage of Cooper & Green which he renamed Eden Park Continental Cars. Ron retired *c.*1971 but his son David continued to expand the business by buying the Bromley Motor Works, formerly Saunders & Abbott, in Wickham Road which he renamed Autobahn.

Saunders & Abbott also has a long history. Like many early motor businesses, Ambrose James Saunders started as a cycle dealer. We first read of him in Station Approach in 1917, and by 1919 he had teamed up with Mr Abbott and was occupying both Tilling's old depot at the side of the Station Hotel and a shed adjoining the fire station in Bromley Road. (It may be due to this close proximity that the fire brigade acquired a motor cycle fire engine.) About 1926 the firm moved from the fire station to the old established garage in Wickham Road now called 'Autobahn'. Originally Price's Bedding Factory, this garage was founded by George Clarke, another cycle dealer turned motor engineer, who had been succeeded in about 1912 by R. & H. Kilner. Mr Saunders collapsed and died outside the *William IV* public house in Elmers End during the war and his surviving partner sold the Wickham Road site to a Mr Harry Epps in 1956.

Private cars were soon a common sight in the village and reports of motor accidents and speeding became commonplace. The Cottage Hospital in its annual report for 1912 commented on the dramatic rise in the number of casualties treated—1,026 compared with 285 the previous year—due to the increase in motor traffic. The High Street was surfaced for the first time in 1905 and virtually the whole of the lower section from Thornton's Corner to the War Memorial was widened and partly straightened between the wars. The 1896 Act laid down a general speed limit of 14 m.p.h. which was increased to 20 m.p.h. in 1903. The present 30 m.p.h. limit in built-up areas dates from the Hore-Belisha Act of 1934 which also author-ised the well-known pedestrian crossings.

In 1930 the Ministry of Transport proposed that what was termed a 'merry go round' one-way system should be introduced where the Croydon Road crossed the Beckenham Road and the Council suggested that the war memorial should be re-sited to a more tranquil position either at Thornton's Corner or in Croydon Road Recreation Ground. The Thornton's Corner site, which had been acquired by the Council from the Post Office when they erected the telephone exchange, was already earmarked for a public lavatory but, more importantly, popular opinion was

65   The Beckenham War Memorial, *c.*1925. When it was erected in 1921 the town's war memorial stood in splendid isolation in the middle of the road and the traffic passed on either side.

very much against moving the memorial so in the end it was decided to allow it to remain whilst enlarging and landscaping the new traffic island to provide a more suitable setting. The island was enlarged still further in 1951. Two other roundabouts in the town, one by the Chinese Garage on the Wickham Road and the other at Elmers End Green, were constructed about the same time. Automatic traffic lights were first installed at each end of Manor Road in the mid-1930s.

Between the wars and before the High Street reached its present congested state there were at least three other places along its length where one could stop and purchase petrol. John Pillin had a garage by the side of the Constitutional Club, Christ Church had leased its newly acquired site in the centre of the High Street to a Mr H.N. Thomson on condition he did not trade on Sundays, and a Mr Dineen sold motor cycles and petrol from a shop still called 'Deen's Garage' just round the corner in Croydon Road.

66 Beckenham's first round-about, seen here in the early 1930s. The roundabout at the War Memorial was constructed in 1930 and the 'Keep Left One Way Only' sign was temporarily fixed to the lamp post.

67 The Chinese Garage and forecourt soon after opening, *c*.1920. The filling station was run to an unusually high standard with attendants dressed in plum coloured chauffeurs' outfits. When the service bay was added, a taxi service for customers was started to take them to the station whilst their cars were being attended to.

68 John Pillin's Garage. The door of the vehicle outside the garage has 'By Appointment' on it, so it is possible that it belonged to Haggers the butchers.

69 This shop in Croydon Road was owned by a Mr Dineen who ran a motor car hire service for many years. The petrol pump on the pavement outside did not disappear until long after the Second World War.

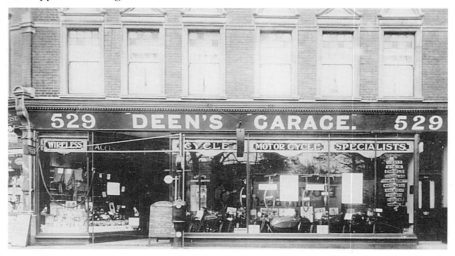

Five

Education

Primary, Secondary and Private

Education was closely tied to the church in early times and we read in the *Life of the learned Dr Assheton, Rector of Beckenham 1677-1711* that the Doctor 'began to raise a Charity School'. Records do not show where the school was nor how long it continued, but it was probably abandoned at, or shortly after, the death of the Rector, as not long after that date we read of children being sent to the master of the village workhouse to receive elementary education.

In 1717 Captain Leonard Bowyer bequeathed £100 to the parish, the interest of which was to be used for teaching four boys belonging to the parish to read and write. For many years, the master of the workhouse received the income of this fund and taught children sent to him by the churchwardens. This was still being done in 1819.

Mary Watson, who died in 1795, left most of her personal estate to the Church. The interest was to pay for the teaching to read and write of so many poor people of Beckenham as were not maintained or supported by the Parish.

The Church of England 'National Society for Educating the Poor' and the British and Foreign School Society were both founded at the beginning of the 19th century. Under these two societies, a number of so-called 'National' and 'British' schools were gradually established in England. The School in Bromley Road, originally known as The National School, was built on a field by St George's church, given by John B. Cator, the Lord of the Manor. In addition to the gift of the site he also provided materials for building a garden round the school and out of work parishioners were employed in levelling the ground and laying out this garden. The work was commenced in April 1818, and the school, a small two-roomed building, opened six months later with 36 boys and 36 girls, most of whom were the children of workers on the local estates. There was a resident school-master and schoolmistress to teach them.

The Abbey School for boys and the nearby Minshull School for girls in Park Road were both founded in 1866 and started what was to become, in late Victorian and Edwardian times, one of Beckenham's most important commercial enterprises. Despite the coincidence of foundation date, we know of no other connection between the two schools whose pupils only met in St Paul's church on Sundays, segregated on opposite sides of the aisle. The Abbey School was quite exceptional both in its size and the quality of its facilities. Starting over Leven's bakery in the

70   The National School in Bromley Road:
built in 1818, enlarged in 1857, extended in
1906 and still going strong. The land was given
by John B. Cator, Lord of the Manor, who also
paid for some of the materials used, giving
work to unemployed men in Beckenham.

High Street it soon moved to a 16-acre gravel pit on the old Copers Cope Farm and acquired an enviable reputation for getting boys into public schools and the Royal Navy. It could claim at least one holder of the Victoria Cross among its former pupils. This was Lt. John Norwood, born at Pembury Lodge, Beckenham in 1876, who won the VC at Ladysmith, but was killed in action in France during the First World War.

At a meeting of the School Board in 1876 it was proposed that additional school accommodation was needed for children in the Alexandra District. There was already a national school in this area but it was exceedingly unpopular and it was said that many parents were sending their children to private schools or to St John's School in Penge, rather than to the existing one which was in such a deplorable state. Mr Albemarle Cator had originally given the land on which the school was built and later he also passed over the buildings to the School Board.

The national system of education dates from Gladstone's Education Act of 1870, which established School Boards all over the country to provide primary education for children between the ages of five and 12 years. This made it possible for the first time to use public funds to provide elementary education. Beckenham became a School District in 1875, and the Beckenham School Board was formed. Although the Act required children to start school at the age of five, a compulsory leaving age had not been established. Directly pupils had learned something of the three R's their parents wanted them to leave school and get a job, although they might only be 11 years old.

The little St James's School at Elmers End was opened in 1880 behind the new church. There are still several people living in the district who attended this school before it closed in May 1930 and all have very happy memories of their time spent there. Miss Hayes, who started teaching there in 1911, was still alive in 1993 at 102 years of age and maintained a keen interest in the area and especially in Marian Vian School which superseded the little church school in 1930.

The Trustees of the Churchfields Charity in 1889 sold part of Bellrope Field to the Beckenham School Board and a school known as Arthur Road School was opened in 1890. The name of the road and the school was changed to Churchfields, after the charity from which the ground had been purchased. The School had four buildings—Infants, Juniors, Seniors and a Special Department. The senior boys later went to Alexandra School and the senior girls stayed until the Secondary Schools re-organisation in 1946 when the pupils were transferred to Marian Vian or Melvin Road in Penge. The Special Department closed and the building was used as an Adult Art Centre.

In 1989, just before its centenary, the School was transferred to a new building on the allotments behind the refuse tip in Churchfields Road, which caused many heated protests at the time from parents and local residents. The old site was redeveloped for housing.

One of the authors (Nancy Tonkin) at this time decided to write a history of Churchfields School and was fortunate, thanks to the Head, Mr Mercer, in being able to borrow on extensive loan all the school archives going back to the opening day on Tuesday 4 November 1890. This complete run of material including log books, entry registers and punishment books proved a fascinated study of the history of a local Beckenham school over a period of nearly a 100 years.

The log books were filled in every day by the head who noted any important event that had taken place. Each book had a clasp and lock and, when the books (filling two tea chests) were collected, there were no keys. This called for a rapid course in lock picking and eventually all the books were opened. Some of them had probably not seen the light of day for 80-90 years.

Although Gladstone's Act of 1870 had provided education for children up to the age of 12 years, the Beckenham School Board had no power to spend public money on secondary schooling. It is an unfortunate fact that, throughout the 19th century, Britain, at that time by far the richest nation in the world, was content to leave the initiative in providing secondary education almost entirely to private enterprise. However, under The Technical Instruction Act of 1889 it became possible

71 St James's School next to the church, *c*.1890. The surroundings were idyllic—a little stream running through the grounds, large trees which gave shade for outdoor summer lessons, and lowing cattle could be heard on the adjacent farm.

to use public funds for secondary education, and it was decided to build the Beckenham Technical Institute in Beckenham Road. The site, a gift from Albemarle Cator, occupied the exact site of the old Clock House, which had been demolished only a few years previously. The foundation stone was laid in July 1899 and the building was formally opened on 4 June 1901. The Institute consisted of the School of Art, the Boys' Day School and the Evening Classes.

The School of Art was particularly successful and survived until the early 1980s, when its premises next to the public library were destroyed by fire. It was continued for a time in the adult education centre at Elmers End but, when that closed, it moved to Bromley.

The population of Beckenham was only about 20,000 when the school was built and the districts of Eden Park and Elmers End were still open fields or private park land. The shops on Clock House Parade near the station had not been built and the Chaffinch brook flowed through a wooded dell where the boys often played. Clock House Road only ran for a very short distance and then ended in fields through which a footpath ran to Elmers End station. The main road from Beckenham to Penge, onto which the School faced, was, even in those days, busy with traffic. There were closed horse buses which followed the route of the present-day No. 227. The traffic in Beckenham Road was disrupted twice a day by cows being driven from Ousley's Dairy in Sidney Road to and from the grazing fields at the end of Clock House Road.

The Beckenham Baths were opened in 1901 and shortly afterwards, owing largely to the efforts of Dr Randell, a member of the Council, swimming was made a compulsory subject in the elementary schools of Beckenham—the first area in the country where this requirement was made. Beckenham had had another first when in 1896 the School Board attracted considerable attention throughout England, deciding that the Union Jack should be hoisted on all the elementary schools on special occasions.

Before the 1870 Act teachers did not need to have done any formal training. They could just open a school and this is what was done in the case of so many of the 'private' schools which abounded in the country. Often the teachers were voluntary and unpaid; only one in 10 was paid. School teachers were not considered very highly. With the passing of the Act and the awareness of the importance of education this rapidly changed.

Extra help came from monitors, sometimes only 10 or 11 years of age, who gave out the slates and helped to keep order. Therefore teachers could cope with very large numbers. Monitors and pupil teachers were paid as little as 3s. 6d. (17½p) per week, they were often 'paid by results' and inspectors would assess their ability not only in imparting knowledge but also in keeping order. Being engaged as a 'Monitor' did not necessarily mean they would be presented as a candidate for 'Pupil Teacher' training.

One of the earliest pupil teachers at Churchfields was Susannah Stannard. The entry for 1 October 1893, the first in the Pupil Teacher Record, was of her being articled and setting out her instruction periods. These were from 8.0 to 9.0 each morning, and her first lesson started on the next day, 2 October. The lessons were Monday, Holy Scripture Liturgy; Tuesday, Arithmetic; Wednesday, Grammar; Thursday, Geography and Music; and on Friday, History and School management.

Each day's lesson was recorded, and signed for by the teacher concerned, as were absences: '15th & 16th February 1894, I excused Susannah Stannard from lessons these two mornings as she was suffering from a severe cold and sore throat'. On Saturday, 14 April 1894 Susannah sat for her first Teachers Examination, and was allowed Monday off. The teachers also had to record absences, and for 5 to 9 November her teacher records, 'I have been unable to give the Pupil Teacher her lessons this week owing to my mother being dangerously ill'. On 1 February: 'I excused the Pupil Teacher from early lessons this morning on account of the weather being so bad'. On 20 April 1895 there was another examination, followed by one day's holiday, and on 10 June her teacher records: 'I was not well enough to give the Pupil Teacher her lessons this morning'. Later that month Susannah had a day off to be confirmed. On 10 July we read, 'The Schools were closed today for fourteen days. The Sanitary Authorities advised by Dr Carpenter the Medical Officer considered it necessary owing to fever.'

14 December 1896: 'Susannah Stannard 4th year Pupil Teacher is absent this week with permission to attend the Scholarship Examination. On 21 September her lessons were disrupted again: 'Schools closed for three weeks to prevent the spread of measles. This by order of the Sanitary Authority'. After the Government Examinations for Pupil Teachers in April 1899, in August she attended the L.S.B. Pupil Training Centre at Hackford Road, Brixton, doing four half days at the centre, and five half days at school with a half-day holiday. This continued until she finished at the beginning of July 1901, when three more Pupil Teachers (Fanny Newman, Emily Wynn and Elsie Mathews) started at the Centre.

Winifred Obee and Lilian Smith were two more Pupil Teachers. They had had a daily lesson 8.00 to 9.00 a.m. or during the lunch hour. Both attended Pupil Teachers Centre at Home and Colonial Training College on Saturdays from 9.00 a.m. to 1.15 p.m. They had homework to do in the evenings. When the school was closed for repairs etc. they had work given to them to do at home.

In 1898 they were doing French lessons and Physiography, an improvement on the standards of 1893 when they were examined in Arithmetic, Geography, Music and singing (although it was 1901 before there was a piano provided for the school), History, English, Penmanship, School Method (i.e. Teaching), Needle-work, Elementary Science, Drawing and Religious Knowledge.

Their examinations were usually held at Bromley Road School. Later they went to the L.S.B. Pupil Teachers Centre at Hackford Road, Brixton, part-time. Pupil teachers were often there for four or five years before going on to full-time training at the age of 19 years. Another Churchfields Pupil teacher—Elizabeth A. Sharpe—taught at Faversham for a period after she qualified. Bessie returned to Churchfields in 1921, where she was a teacher for 29 years. Much later in life, after she retired from teaching, she was to become Nancy Tonkin's stepmother.

Balfour's Education Act of 1901 changed the status of the school because it placed full responsibility for providing secondary education on the county councils. Beckenham, by establishing the Day School, had in a sense anticipated the Act.

72 Churchfields Road School, *c.*1910. Note the tiered rows towards the back of the classroom.

The Beckenham Technical Day School became the Beckenham County Secondary School, the first of its kind in the county of Kent, and possibly in the country.

Fees were charged, and to begin with they were £1 15s. per term for sons of Beckenham ratepayers and £2 2s. for others. From the start there had been 16 scholarship places awarded by the Local Authority, but from 1907 it became obligatory to provide 25 per cent free places in all maintained county secondary schools. These were competed for in an annual scholarship examination and fee-payers also had to pass an entrance examination. This remained the system of entry until 1944.

Baden Powell founded the Boy Scout movement in 1907 and, shortly after this, the Technical School formed a troop under the leadership of Mr R.W. Clark. It was the 1st Beckenham Troop and grew to a membership of about fifty. However, as other troops connected with the churches began to appear, the numbers in the school troop started to decline and it was disbanded.

Once the war was over, the local authorities began looking for a site to build a larger school and the St Arvan's site in Penge was acquired in 1925 and building commenced in 1929. The School remained at Penge until January 1968, when it was transferred to the new larger buildings at Eden Park and was renamed Langley Park School for Boys. After 1931, when the school moved to Penge, the building in Beckenham Road was used as a technical school until in 1955 this moved to new buildings in Bromley. It was then used as overflow accommodation by the Alexandra Secondary (formerly Senior) School for Boys until in 1968 they in turn moved to their new building near Kelsey Park. Kelsey Park School, as it is now called, traces its ancestry back to the Alexandra Boys School which opened in 1875 in a tiny building with only one teacher. It adjoined the London and Provincial Steam Laundry whose dense black smoke often filled the classrooms and left the occupants with a most disagreeable smell. In winter the ink often froze in the ink wells. The Technical School building still survives today, its exterior virtually unchanged, under the name of 'The Studio', and is used as a council-run arts and media venue.

It had soon become obvious that more secondary schools were required and it was decided to build two more. Lennard Road was to become The Beckenham County School for Girls, whilst the Balgowan Road School became a combined Boys' and Girls' Central School, the first co-ed school in Kent. Before either of the new schools was opened, the First World War had started and the buildings were requisitioned as Red Cross Military Hospitals, being returned to the Education Committee in 1919. They opened for their original purpose in September of that year.

Miss Fox was headmistress at Lennard Road for the first 24 years. Her pupils were known as 'Miss Fox's young ladies'. She was an extremely strict disciplinarian both with the staff as well as the children. Miss Fox retired just before the end of the Second World War and the atmosphere became considerably more relaxed. No longer were the staff expected to wear long skirts, long sleeves, and high necks. The pupils wore beige lisle stockings instead of the original black ones and the younger girls were allowed ankle socks—a great concession while clothes rationing was still in operation.

73 The County School for Boys, Beckenham and Penge, *c*.1935. The new school, a few yards across the Beckenham border, was ready for occupation at the beginning of 1931. Mr Sidney Gammon, a graduate in History from New College, Oxford, became headmaster in the autumn term that year and remained until he was killed, with his wife and son, in a bombing raid on 23 October 1940.

74   Miss Fox and the prefects in 1924. Pupils had to wear black stockings both summer and winter and the square-necked blouses ensured that necks were washed daily! Gym slips had to be a regulation four inches above the knees.

75   Lennard Road staff in 1946. The staff in Miss Fox's day were expected to wear dresses or blouses with high necks and long sleeves. Dress became less formal after the war.

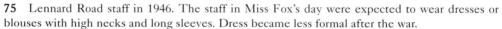

One of the really significant changes in council-provided education concerned the development of secondary schools. Under Fisher's Education Act of 1918 a duty was imposed on local authorities to provide secondary schools in which at least 20 per cent of the places were to be free. This was not intended to mean secondary education for everyone, but rather for those who, regardless of financial circumstances, showed they could benefit from it. Right up to 1945 the majority of children still attended full-time schooling at elementary schools to the age of 14—raised from 13 under Fisher's Act.

At the beginning of the century most boys' scholastic ambition was London Matriculation at the age of 16, and very few stayed on at school after this. There has been a vast expansion in the sixth form since those days. Many were going on to university but, until the introduction of state grants for students, it had not been easy for the average county school child to go to university unless he/she could win a major scholarship. Another important development in education came about as a result of a need to provide less-academic children with a more 'practical' kind of secondary school. This was called the Central School, which laid emphasis on commercial training, technical training, music and art. The name disappeared after the Second World War but the concept lived on in the guise of the Secondary Technical School.

The Boys' School at Kent House Road became Kent Wood Secondary Modern School for Boys, then Royston Primary School and is now partly used as an Adult Education Centre. The Lennard Road site became Cator Park Secondary Modern School for Girls. Balgowan Central had its boys' section closed with the re-organisation of schools within the borough in 1946. The girls' section was extended to take girls from Bromley Road and other schools and continued there as a Secondary Modern School until it moved to the empty Lennard Road building in 1959.

The Girls' Secondary School at Marian Vian became a mixed school known as Spring Park Lower until it finally closed in July 1979. That building is now an adult education centre. The Junior Mixed and Infant Departments of Marian Vian became a joint Primary School in 1982 and in 1992 celebrated its Diamond Jubilee.

Stewart Fleming Primary School opened in September 1939 to take the children living near Birkbeck station and it was named after the Rev. Stewart Fleming who, whilst minister at Elm Road Baptist Church, was for many years chairman of the Beckenham School Board.

In late Victorian and Edwardian times private schools of all shapes and sizes were so numerous in Beckenham that it would not be out of place to describe education as a most important commercial undertaking. It was an occupation which appeared very early in the development of the town. Many were too small to survive. At one time there were eight in Mackenzie Road alone. However, of the larger ones, some of which were also boarding schools, several have survived and are still thriving today.

A notable survivor is the well-known girls' school, St Christopher's, which opened in Perth Road in 1893. After moving first to Rectory Road and then to The Avenue it merged in 1926 with another school, 'The Hall' in Bromley Road. Enid Blyton was

76 The Hall in Bromley Road was probably built by the Cator family in the 18th century, but very little is known of its early history. Peter Cator, who played a prominent part in the development of the Cator Estate, lived there until his death in 1873 and in 1878 Charles Cator was in residence. A school was started there in 1893 and St Christopher's took over in 1926 and celebrated its centenary in 1993.

77 A schoolroom at Raymont School, Shortlands, *c*.1910. Raymont School off Bromley Road was a small boarding school for girls.

perhaps St Christopher's most famous pupil. She attended between 1907 and 1917 and was a prize winner in 1915 and Head Girl for her two final years. It is interesting to note that she probably would have been refused admission to The Hall school prior to the amalgamation as it catered exclusively for the daughters of gentlemen and professional men; tradesmen's daughters, however wealthy, were not accepted. One pupil was asked to leave when it was discovered her father was a local pharmacist.

The Eden Park School is also unusual as it was not founded until 1938 in a semi-detached house a few doors from its present premises to which it moved the following year. It prospered by providing private education during the war years when most of its competitors had either closed or moved to the country.

Other girls' schools were Raymont in Shortlands Grove, run by the Kendall sisters, and Kepplestone School.

Kepplestone School for the Daughters of Gentlemen was at Kelsey Manor until that building became too dilapidated in 1908 when the school moved to Overbury Avenue.

Some schools simply closed down during the war years, Clare House at 22 Oakwood Avenue, Beckenham being a case in point. This school, which was founded in 1896, took boys as day or boarding pupils, and prepared them to enter a Public School or the Royal Navy. It finally failed in 1970 owing to financial difficulties, but the name is carried on by a school in the State sector which opened on the same site.

78 Minshull House, in Park Road, *c*.1910. Founded in 1866, it was one of the oldest private schools in the area. The school was evacuated to Woolacombe in Devon during the Second World War and there were specially reduced war-time fees. In 1965 it was pulled down and redeveloped for residential purposes.

79 The rear view of Kepplestone School, Overbury Avenue, just before the First World War.

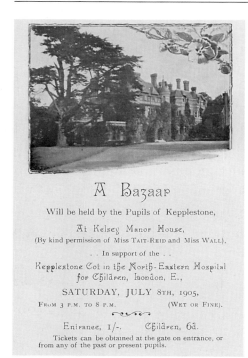

A Bazaar

Will be held by the Pupils of Kepplestone,

At Kelsey Manor House,
(By kind permission of Miss Tait-Reid and Miss Wall),

. . In support of the . .

Kepplestone Cot in the North-Eastern Hospital
for Children, London, E.,

SATURDAY, JULY 8th, 1905,

From 3 p.m. to 8 p.m.   (Wet or Fine).

Entrance, 1/-.   Children, 6d.

Tickets can be obtained at the gate on entrance, or
from any of the past or present pupils.

80 An advert for a Bazaar at Kepplestone in 1905. The bazaar was held while the school was still at Kelsey Manor. The exorbitant entrance fee of one shilling would have kept many of Beckenham's population away considering that, for the majority of working-class men, wages were less than £2 per week in those days.

81 The Abbey School, in Southend Road, *c*.1910. The buildings were purpose-built and in the dormitories each boy had a separate cubicle. By the 1930s central heating and electric light were installed throughout. The grounds provided ample playing fields and there was a riding school attached.

Craven College for boys was one of the larger private schools, housed first in Beckenham Place and latterly at Elmer Lodge near the junction of Dunbar Avenue and Eden Park Avenue, where the magistrate Edward Adams once lived.

Albemarle College, founded in 1879 at No. 10 Beckenham Road as a girls' school, was reorganised in 1930 as a modern Secretarial and Tutorial College. Courses of secretarial and commercial training were provided for students of both sexes with previous high school or public school education. Coaching was given for Professional and Civil Service Examinations. The site is now occupied by the modern fire and ambulance station.

The Grange Preparatory School for Boys, 25 Wickham Road, founded in 1926, prepared boys from the ages of seven to 14 for all public schools. There was a separate junior department for boys of five to seven years. The classrooms were lofty and well-ventilated, and they had a large sports ground, near Park Langley. In 1930 the school prospectus advertised 'large sports ground in Open Country'.

Woodbrook, in Hayne Road, was a school run on the most up-to-date lines, providing for the education of children from nursery to college. The rooms were large and airy; there was a large garden for work and games, and a sandpit for the little ones. There was a nursery department which provided educational occupations for children under five, and the work from kindergarten up was carefully graded. Individual attention was given to each child and, to ensure this, the classes were kept small. Very successful work was done in preparing pupils for advanced examinations. Senior girls were prepared for the Oxford School Certificate and London Matriculation, and boys for entrance to public and preparatory schools. The most modern methods were adopted throughout the school. There was a laboratory, gymnasium, and garden. Hockey, netball, tennis and swimming were taught. The principals were especially interested in the 'backward' child. The school closed in the 1960s and has been replaced by a council-run school which opened in 1970 bearing the same name and still specialising in children with special needs.

St Olaf's school was on the corner of Cedars Road and Croydon Road. It opened at the beginning of the 20th century but did not survive beyond the outbreak of the First World War.

Two post-Second World War developments deserve special mention. In 1950 a Roman Catholic Infants School opened in the old Shortlands House on the Bromley Road, previously a hotel. It rapidly expanded to include older pupils and by 1958 had become a full scale secondary grammar school. It was then renamed

82 One of the football pitches at the Abbey School, *c.*1910. The extensive grounds enabled the school to have more than one pitch for their soccer matches.

83 Clare House School in Oakwood Avenue. The message on the reverse of this card, posted in 1905, reads: 'Hope you all got back safely from the station without meeting the ticket collector. Love from Dad.' Presumably the writer could afford to send his sons to a private school but not to pay their dues to the railway company!

84   Craven College in Dunbar Avenue just before the First World War. There was a polo ground at the rear which was said to be one of the finest in the country.

85   St Olaf's School at 2, Cedars Road around 1910. This small mixed private school obviously catered for all ages and whole families were sent there.

the Bishop Challoner School in honour of the Roman Catholic bishop of that name (1691-1781) who was in charge of the faith in London and the Home Counties during the 18th century.

No one can fail to notice that the St George's Road car park is periodically crowded with continental coaches, a sign that English language courses have become yet another growth activity in Beckenham. These visitors are mainly destined for short courses conducted in church halls and other venues in the district. The King's School of English, almost opposite the Public Library, is, however, a fully accredited school with an international reputation. It opened in 1966, one of a group of three schools, the others being in Bournemouth and Oxford, and takes its name from its founder, a Mr King.

Besides these there were numerous dancing schools, secretarial and business training schools. The Art School with its yellow door on Church Hill, now a conservative club, features prominently in the newspapers of the day. A very successful School of Art was started in 1901 at the Technical Institute and later moved further along Beckenham Road opposite Elm Road. It was burnt down in the early 1980s and not rebuilt. There was a branch of this school for many years at 80, Croydon Road. The School gained great prominence in examinations in art by the success of its pupils, who took some of the chief awards. There were two sections, senior and junior, and all branches of art were taught.

There was a music college in The Parade facing Beckenham Junction with an impressive list of professors. The Royal Academy of Dancing & Music was at The Studio in the High Street; Doris Nichols taught ballroom dancing at The Assembly Rooms, whilst Joan Baron held her classes at the *Eden Park Hotel.*

Adult evening classes were held at various schools in the borough and in particular at the Evening Education Centre in Beckenham Road at the old Technical Institute building. Many of the classes now could almost be listed under leisure rather than education for they cover such a wide selection of subjects from purely educational, through the whole range of art and handicrafts, family and local history, to keep-fit and dancing.

Balfour's Act of 1901 started the system of publicly maintained secondary schools in this country, but the second great milestone in its history was R.A. Butler's Act of 1944. It made secondary education for all to the age of 15 compulsory and free, and although there was nothing in the Act to prevent county authorities from setting up comprehensive secondary schools, the general pattern was that of selection at the age of 11-plus for either Grammar, Technical or Modern Schools. Later the 11-plus examination was abolished and selective schools ceased to be.

In the 1930s there were gradual improvements in the school health and welfare services. It was a requirement that children be medically examined three times during their school life, and, though the medicals were perfunctory affairs lasting only a few minutes and were too infrequent to spot unhealthy conditions at an early stage, they could result in treatment, however belated, that might otherwise never be given. The clinic block at the new town hall was unusual and forward-looking. It was a complete child welfare and health centre and covered all ages from ante-natal care to senior school children. In 1933 about one-third of children at council schools attended school clinics. Nearly half of these were at the dental clinic. Under a newly introduced scheme children could receive daily at school one-third of a pint of fresh milk for a charge of one halfpenny (old money).

Dr T. Phillips Cole, M.O.H. for Beckenham, reported in 1933 that too many children were underweight, 'a serious problem if it is not put right', but unemployment among parents was not seen as a significant factor in this. By 1936 the immunisation programme had reduced diphtheria cases in Beckenham to only five, against 122 for scarlet fever. By then over half of the children in local schools were taking daily milk.

What is perhaps remembered most clearly about school medical matters from those days were the regular appearances of a nurse who went through every child's head in search of lice. She was affectionately called 'Nitty Norah'.

We should not leave education without mentioning punishments, now along with discipline firmly a thing of the past. Here once again we have the archives of Churchfields School to delve into.

'Spare the rod and spoil the child.' This sentiment has now gone out of fashion, and while some of us may think the pendulum has swung too far the other way, there is no doubt our grandparents would have been shocked at our present system of actually rewarding some wrongdoers. Nevertheless, although punishment at school was seen as a necessary aid to keeping discipline, it was carried out within very careful guidelines. Children would or could be caned for minor misdemeanours.

An entry in the Boys' Log Book in 1910 states: 'A copy of the following regulation was handed to each assistant master for their guidance: Assistant Teachers and Pupil Teachers are absolutely prohibited from inflicting corporal punishment of any description. The Head Teacher shall be held directly and strictly responsible for every punishment of the kind.' This was signed by the Clerk of the Local Education Authority.

In April 1914 the Beckenham Education Committee published an extract from the Committee's Regulations on School Discipline and Corporal Punishment. This laid down the rules under which a child could be punished at school, and a copy of these rules was pasted on the front pages of both the Boy's Department and the Junior Mixed and Infants Department Punishment Books.

(A)   Head Teachers are to use every endeavour to reduce all forms of punishment to the minimum compatible with the welfare of the children and the school, and are not in any case to inflict corporal punishment (save for grave moral offences) until other methods have been tried and failed.

(B)   Head Teachers are held responsible for all punishment, corporal or other punishment, but they are allowed, where they think necessary to delegate during pleasure the power to inflict slight punishment to such of their associates as they consider to be fit and proper persons to be entrusted with that power. The power of delegation is limited to cases of assistants who have obtained their parchments. In a Mixed school under a master, any necessary corporal punishment of girls must be inflicted by an assistant mistress duly delegated by the head teacher. The head teachers, who, under this section, either give to, or withdraw from their assistants the power to inflict slight punishment, must do so in writing, and must note the same in the log-book.

(C)   A cane or other instrument of punishment authorised by the Committee is provided for each department, and when an assistant entrusted with the power of inflicting punishment has need for exercising that power, the assistant must obtain from the head teacher the instrument of punishment and the punishment book, and, after inflicting the punishment, and entering and signing the same in the book, must forthwith return both the instrument of punishment and the book to the head teacher, who must initial the entry. The head teacher is not to use any discretion in refraining from entering cases of corporal punishment.

(D)   In Infants Departments it is left to the discretion of the head teacher to permit the use of the open hand, instead of the cane, as an instrument of punishment, but such substituted punishment must be recorded in the punishment book.

(E)   The punishment book is to be preserved for five years after being filled.

(F)   All irregular, cruel, and excessive corporal punishment is absolutely prohibited, and in the event of an assistant breaking any of these rules, the head teacher is required to report immediately the same direct to the Clerk of the Committee.

(G)   All cases of cruel corporal punishment will entail dismissal.

(H)   Head Teachers must secure, that throughout the school, special caution is exercised in the cases of delicate and nervous children.

(I)   All blows by the hand, cuffs, boxing the ear, striking on any part of the head, shakings, or any other irregular modes of inflicting corporal punishment are strictly forbidden to all teachers.

This was a very comprehensive set of rules, and any case of cruel punishment could be punished by the dismissal of the teacher concerned. The school started to use the punishment books at the end of September 1914, and the log book records in that month:

In accordance with the Regulation of the Education Committee re Corporal Punishment dated April 1914 all the Certified Teachers in this Department, have power to inflict slight corporal punishment 'with the open hand'. Permission has accordingly been given to seven members of staff.

The punishment book for the Junior Mixed and Infants Department recorded all punishments up to 2 June 1937, with just one further entry in March 1939. During this period of 25 years a total of 151 children was recorded as having been punished, which works out at one child every two months. The reader may wonder what punishments were carried out in the Infants Department, and how old or rather how young were the children. It is all carefully recorded.

While children as young as five years could be punished, only four under six years of age are reported in all that time. In 1915, for kicking a boy on the leg after warnings and taking a little girl's hat, a lad was punished with a 'slap on leg with open hand'. In 1920 another five-year-old lad was punished for 'stubbornness and bad temper', with 'one tap on hand with teachers own hand', and in 1921 for 'deliberate disobedience', a child received a 'slap on arm'. In the same year a five-and-a-half-year-old child had both hands slapped for 'coming in late as he was playing on the road'.

As the children got older the entries increase, but still only 23 six-year-old children were punished in 25 years. The punishment in nearly every case was either being slapped on the arm, on the hands, or on the leg. The crimes were mostly constant disobedience, a case of what we would now call grievous bodily harm, i.e. sticking a pin in a boy's leg, or stealing and lying to the teacher. Only one boy had a stroke of the cane on each hand, and that was for 'dirty behaviour in the playground'.

The bulk of the entries concern boys of seven and eight years of age, the cane was used more often, with slapping on the hands, arms or legs still being the punishment for many offences. After June 1924 the cane was done away with, and replaced with a 'flat ruler', which was used from then on for the more serious offences: 'Application of ruler to both arms' or 'Application of ruler to hands and legs'.

Out of the 151 children punished, five were girls. The youngest was six years three months, who received three slaps on her arm for scribbling in a reading book. Only three girls were caned, and the severest punishment was one stroke on each hand for 'dirty behaviour in the lavatory'.

The Boys' Department punishment book, like the Junior Mixed and Infants, starts in 1914 but goes through to 1958. Here, bearing in mind we are dealing with lads from eight to 13 years, the cane is used more often: usually one or two strokes, sometimes three and, very rarely—probably not more than about a dozen times, (in 44 years)—four strokes. At one point at the end of 1914 there was an outbreak of climbing on the school walls; three lads on the same day got the maximum of four strokes for this, which effectively put a stop to that problem, and it did not arise again. On another day two boys were given four strokes for 'filthy habits' while 'tearing a reading book' also warranted four strokes. Two boys caught stealing were also given four strokes.

'Blots on book' was always good for one stroke and sometimes two, but woe betide you, if you tried to rub the blots out, that earned you three strokes, as did 'blowing snuff into the eyes of several boys'. 'Discharging fireworks in the playground', two strokes. By the early 1920s two strokes was becoming the norm for many offences.

In March 1923 a new punishment appears: 'slight whipping', and whenever a boy was whipped the teacher was always careful to call it a 'slight' whipping. This sounds dreadful and it is not known exactly what the punishment was or what was used. It could not have been too bad because it was often accompanied by either one or two strokes of the cane. At the end of 1925 a boy was given a slight whipping at the parents' request for 'doing damage to allotments'. No more slight whippings were carried out after July 1931.

The boys were not to escape the flat ruler, although it was not used until 1942. Worse things were in store, however, and in 1949, for 'interfering with staff bicycles, letting down tyres etc.', the punishment was a spanking with a slipper.

In all just over 1,300 punishments to boys and girls were recorded in the 44 years the book was kept, which works out at about thirty incidences per year.

From January 1925 until the middle of 1931, girls' punishments were also recorded in the boys' punishment book. The girls, from nine to 11, were not treated so harshly as the boys. 'Slight slap on back of hand', 'slapping on legs' or, as was more often the case, 'slapping an arm' appear a lot more often than caning. When a girl was caned it was usually one stroke, and never more than two strokes.

Six

Industry and Commerce

Shops, Factories and Tradesmen

The clearest early glimpse we can get of the commercial life of Beckenham is provided by Pigot's 1839 *Kent Directory* in which 33 tradesmen are listed. Thirteen years later, when work had started on building the Crystal Palace in the parish, the population had increased by over a quarter, and about half of the original tradesmen are still in business. Notable newcomers are a surgeon, a chemist and no fewer than four beer retailers.

There was the West Kent brewery which was started by James Learner in Upper Elmers End Road in the mid-19th century. The going rate for beer then was: India pale ale at 1s. 6d. a gallon, stout at 1s. 4d. a gallon and 'porter' ale, just a shilling. The brewery was run by Pontiflex and Hall for 30 years and they mixed their hops in Elmers End, and were very proud of their product. Soon after their opening, they announced that they had 'sunk a deep artesian well and have much pleasure in stating that the water obtained from there is pronounced by an eminent doctor to be of the purest quality. From this water all our beers are produced'. And of the building itself they said, 'It is constructed on the most proven modern principles and is particularly adapted for the production of high-class family ales'. The brewery had a number of owners before closing in 1908 when the building was taken over by Kempton's Pies. The old building was demolished in the 1960s and the site is now a block of council flats.

Beckenham village industries were the smithies, millers, carpenters and masons. The blacksmiths, beside shoeing the horses, would repair the farm tools and machinery, and assist the local wheelwright. Farming remained an important occupation until the housing developments of the 1920s swallowed up the last remnants of open country. Until this time there were fields in the centre of Beckenham and along the Croydon Road, and it was nothing unusual for traffic to be disrupted as cows were driven from their grazing fields to the dairy. In the memory of living residents the site of the Village Way car park was occupied by farm buildings where once a week could be heard the squealing of pigs as they met their fate and a well known post card shows cows grazing in a field with the building now occupied by the HSBC bank visible just across the road.

Another local industry was brick making and the quarrying of sand and gravel. This industry expanded enormously as building in the area took off. There were several large brickfields in Beckenham and the surrounding areas. Still conspicuous

86   Upper Elmers End Road showing the *Rising Sun*, and the brewery with its tall chimney a little further down the road.

87   A forge in Burnhill Road, *c.*1900. The blacksmith would also sometimes make large steel hoops with which the children could play in the uncongested streets of bygone days.

today is the gravel pit site in which Beckenham Station is built and which necessitated a diversion in the High Street. William Pitt introduced a tax on bricks in 1784 and immediately, to avoid this tax, bricks were made larger until in 1803 the tax was doubled if the brick was made bigger than 10 x 3 x 5 inches before firing. The size could be reduced by up to 10 per cent in the kiln. The tax was abolished in 1850. Several brickyards had opened to exploit the local clay and supply builders. The Mid-Kent Brickworks in Worsley Bridge Road hit the headlines in 1885 when five workers were killed in a boiler explosion.

Many of the businesses in the new town were started by people who came from other parts of the country, attracted by the opportunities arising from the growing population, and the active building programme. A particularly good example is that of Syme & Duncan Ltd, a firm of builders founded in 1870. James Syme was a Scotsman and skilled carpenter, employed in 1870 by a firm which was constructing St Mary's vicarage at Shortlands. The firm went into liquidation and James as foreman was asked if he could finish the job himself. This he did with the help of a friend, William Duncan, a fellow tradesman, also from Scotland. With this success behind them the partners went on to build houses in Southend Road, Rectory Road and elsewhere, it is believed on a speculative basis. Before the houses were started it was necessary to dig a well, and the gravel excavated in doing this was used in the house construction. In 1885 the firm was able to lease its former premises in Blakeney Road. One of the largest of its early successes was the construction of the parade of shops at Clock House in 1904. Until a few years ago Syme and Duncan Ltd were one of the oldest surviving businesses in Beckenham but its 1885 premises in Blakeney Road have now been replaced by a row of town houses.

Henry Copeland, grandfather of the late Rob Copeland, the local historian, was yet another example. He came from Sleaford in Lincolnshire in 1862 with his brother William and obtained employment as a carpenter. By 1874 he was able to set up in business on his own as a builder and undertaker from premises in the High Street. In those days it was not unusual for a builder also to be an undertaker since he had the wood for the coffins and his labourers could dig the graves. Rob Copeland was the third generation to run the business. He died in 1988, but the business still survives though now it is owned by the CWS.

At the beginning of the 19th century Beckenham's few shops were small and run by tradesmen catering for the needs of the villagers. All this changed in the 1860s and '70s when Beckenham must have had the air of a boom town. To meet the needs of the rapidly growing population on the new estates, parades of shops were built between the church and station as well as at the lower end of Albemarle Road. Development was not confined to the town centre. Shopping parades were built on the main roads in places where there were already commercial premises such as Westgate and Beckenham Roads or in the vicinity of a railway station as at Clock House.

The more typical Victorian business was small and family owned by people who at first lived over the 'shop' and usually lasted for only two or three generations. Hitt's, Wine and Spirit Merchants, is an example of this. William Hitt came from Somerset and started his business in 1864, though he first appears in the *Bromley*

88   The parade of shops at Clock House, *c.*1914. Proximity to customers was not of prime importance when tradesmen were expected to wait upon the gentry, and poorer customers usually lived in humbler dwellings in the immediate vicinity. The parade was built by the local builder Syme & Duncan in 1904.

89   Hitt's Stores in the High Street, *c.*1904. Hitt's shop itself has changed beyond recognition but, as is so often the case, the upper storey has survived virtually unchanged to this day.

Directory for 1878. In 1915 he passed on the business to his son, Frederick, who retired and sold it about 1934.

Firms from outside the area opened branches in Beckenham and some of the earliest examples of these were branches of local businesses based in Bromley, such as Weeks, the ironmongers, and Howard's, the grocers, who built the premises at present occupied by the HSBC Bank. Aylings the Bromley shoe shop founded in 1790, also opened two branches in Beckenham and only closed in 1992.

Sainsbury's was soon followed by the Home and Colonial whilst Howard's was replaced by the International Stores. As the

I am a solicitor for

HOWARD'S STORES, Ltd.

who sell the BEST OF EVERYTHING
See what I have to say—

P. T. O.

90 Howard's was unusual in being sited away from the station but its example was to be followed by the first national multiple to appear, Sainsbury's.

91 Sainsbury's opened in 1915 in the High Street on the site of Gordon House, which had stood next to the Old Wood House, still visible on the left of the picture.

inter-war period wore on they were joined by Boot's, Timothy White's, MacFisheries, Woolworth's, Dewhurst's, and Montague Burton's. These were all situated along the High Street, having taken advantage of the demolition of the old domestic properties such as the Rectory, the Manor House and Village Place and the proximity of the large new housing estate being built by J.R. Davies on their former grounds.

Between the wars additional parades were built at Eden Park, Elmers End, Croydon Road and Langley Park to serve the new housing estates. They usually consisted of smallish shops designed to cater for customers within walking distance, at a time before motor cars had become such a universal possession.

92   A parade of shops in Croydon Road, *c.*1939, which was built between the new Bramerton and Whitmore Roads.

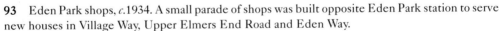

93   Eden Park shops, *c.*1934. A small parade of shops was built opposite Eden Park station to serve new houses in Village Way, Upper Elmers End Road and Eden Way.

94 Adam's Drapery, c.1910. The drapers and milliners in the High Street, who stocked everything a good needlewoman might require, provided chairs for their many customers as well.

The old shops may not have had the efficiency of the modern supermarket but they had an atmosphere which lives on in the memory of older people. For example, Adams the drapers, where you had to bend your head and mind the step, and your money went whizzing across the shop to the cash desk by pulling the handle of the overhead railway.

A trade which was very prominent before the First World War was nursery gardening. The spectacular bedding schemes which were a feature of the Crystal Palace grounds stimulated great rivalry amongst the owners of the numerous large gardens and there was a brisk trade supplying those who from lack of time or inclination had neglected their own production. All have now disappeared. Only the Eden Park Garden Centre remains.

Beckenham is primarily a residential area with its not inconsiderable industry confined to its northern and western outskirts at Elmers End, Churchfields, Kent House Road and Lower Sydenham. Since the war London has become too expensive

95   Castle's Nursery opposite Elmers End Cemetery in 1920. This family concern was founded by John Alfred Castle in 1906 through the generosity of his former employer who provided, and later sold him, both land and house. The only condition was no Sunday trading and this instruction could be seen carved in stone by the side of the door. It was observed until closure in 1999.

96   Popham's General Stores, around 1920, on Church Hill. The tiling at the front of the shop can still be seen today.

and congested compared with other parts of the country, and change of ownership or reorganisation has often resulted in a re-siting elsewhere. As a result the manufacturing of electrical equipment (Muirhead 1895; Small Electric Motors 1914), leather (Kohnstamm), adhesives, office equipment (Twinlock 1920), etc., which featured so prominently before the war have been replaced by trading and administrative activities. For example, a much reduced Muirheads has moved from Elmers End to Penge, Small Electric Motors from Churchfields Road to Lower Sydenham, whilst important new activities such as Barclays Registrars are now based at Clock House.

Small Electric Motors started operations at Churchfields Road at the beginning of the First World War. They moved down from the City over a weekend by horse and cart. Apparently the cart wheels kept getting stuck in the tram lines along the Old Kent Road and at Lewisham. The premises they took over were originally a pin and needle factory and for years afterwards these were still being swept off the floor. They now operate from Kangley Bridge Road, just inside the Beckenham boundary.

Percy Jones & Co., makers of ribbons, carbons and filing systems, started making Twinlock loose-leaf ledgers in Cheapside in 1910 as agents for the American inventor, and moved to Elmers End in 1920, next to Muirheads. These two businesses between them employed a huge workforce and it was a sad day for the district when they moved away.

The Wellcome Foundation, one of the most important drug manufacturers in the world, was founded in 1880 by two American pharmacists. The Company bought Langley Court in South Eden Park Road in 1921 and opened their research laboratories on the site. They were taken over by Glaxo and then by Smith Kline, so that only a small remnant remains on the site.

97 Aerial view of the Elmers End industrial site. Taken in the 1980s, it shows the Muirhead and Twinlock factories, now replaced by a Tesco supermarket. The building in the centre foreground was for many years Ackerman's bakery. In the background can be seen the branch line to Addiscombe, now replaced by the new Tramlink.

98 Thornton's Corner, *c.*1913. Their sun awnings show how diverse were the services offered and indicate why the area is now called Thornton's Corner.

Publishing in Beckenham is synonymous with the Thornton family. Thomas W. Thornton was the owner of the stationers and booksellers business on the corner of the High Street which bears his name. He purchased the *Beckenham Journal* from its founder, William Malyon, who lived in Victor Road on the Alexandra Estate. He was a director of the London printers, Malyon & Watson, who are assumed to have printed the early editions of the newspaper which first appeared in September 1876.

The *Beckenham Journal* began its life as a 24-page monthly booklet costing 1d. The increasing population, as the Cator and Shortlands estates were built, turning, in the space of one generation, the village into a commuter town, meant that by the early 1880s *The Journal* could be issued as a weekly newspaper.

Tom Thornton, who came from Norwood, walked daily to and from the Beckenham shop. He installed a steam-driven printing press behind his stationer's shop and in 1882 started to produce the paper weekly. This was later moved to a purpose-built works behind the shops on the corner of Kelsey Park and Manor Roads, the editorial work being carried out in what has been described as an attached conservatory, until in 1954 one of the corner shops was acquired for the purpose.

When he died in 1933 Tom Thornton had been confined to a wheelchair for some time. He was succeeded as editor by E.J. Dark, who retired during the war, to be replaced by Victor Thornton who remained in the position until his death in 1963. In 1955 control of the paper was sold to the *Kentish Times* who have continued to keep the title alive, though the printing works was almost immediately closed and production transferred to Sidcup.

The Beckenham & Penge Advertiser, an off shoot of the *Croydon Advertiser*, also had a weekly issue.

Thornton's brought out a *Beckenham Directory* which in 1885 sold for one shilling (5p). Besides being printers and publishers, they were listed in 1906 as stationers, billposting and advertising agents, bookbinders, newsagent, artist's colourman, fancy qarehouseman, railway and steamship ticket agent, entertainment agent etc. and coped with piano tuning and picture framing. They also ran a lending library from their shop in the High Street. Beckenham did not have its own library until 1939.

Walter Andrew Mathew died aged 92 in January 1968. From 1898-1910, when he left the district, he ran Beckenham's first garage in the High Street, near *The George*, but later moved to larger premises, also in the High Street. The first motor-car-related businesses to be listed in the directories appear in *Thornton's Directory* for 1902 (see pp. 52 to 56).

Holdsworth's, the well-known lightweight cycle manufacturers, started their business between the wars in Lennard Road before moving to their factory in the old banana warehouse at Lullington Road, Penge. For many years they had a shop on the corner of Barnmead Road. A range of bicycle carriers was made exclusively for the Holdsworth Co. by Tonard Brazing Co. Ltd which started making them in Blandford Road, Beckenham in 1960 before moving to Croydon, where they became one of the largest manufacturers of cycle carriers in the country.

Ernest Walter Payne founded his jeweller's shop in Penge in 1899 and then opened a branch in Bromley market square 11 years later. The Beckenham shop in the High Street was not opened until 1932 but after 70 years is still a thriving concern.

The Pearce family of Elmers End for many years swept the borough's chimneys before the Clean Air Act stopped coal fires. Generations of the family have been sweeping chimneys since 1640 and must surely be one of the oldest family businesses in the country. They have been much in demand to kiss brides and New Year revellers in order to bring them good luck.

David Greig the grocer lived at The Red House in Southend Road. It was unusual to have a Sainsbury's store and a David Greig's in the same area but in Beckenham there was a David Greig shop at the bottom of Mackenzie Road before it was bombed in the 1940s.

We have mentioned local farms and the milk delivery but without a doubt the United Dairies (now known as Unigate) was the most prolific. At the start of the Second World War Beckenham still had private dairies such as Ousley's, Herbert's, Ironside's and Overton's, but the United Dairies had seven shops in the borough and their distributing depot was in the High Street where the entrance to the former Safeways is now. The South Suburban Co-op and the Express Dairy both delivered milk in the area but the U.D. took most of the trade. All their premises had very distinctive tiled shop fronts. Their deliveries were made by horse and cart and the horses knew the route better than many of the milkmen. If a milkman stopped for too long to talk to a customer the horse would just plod on to the next house. Because of the horses the distributing depot needed stabling, tack rooms and harness rooms, fodder lofts and a resident stable man. The vet made a weekly visit to see that all the Welsh Cobs were in good condition. These horses took part in the annual Commercial Horse Parade held in Regents Park and rarely returned without several awards. The electric milk floats which we know today were introduced soon after the war ended. Fortunately Beckenham is not too hilly because these new floats with their heavy batteries had problems when they went up hill, and replacement batteries were frequently needed to enable them to complete the round.

It is impossible to give full details of the numerous businesses which have been carried on in Beckenham over the past 150 odd years. Many were very small affairs trading from the front room of a house, such as sweet shops and grocers in the side streets. Many women in the poorer part of the village would start up their own laundry and take in washing from the large houses at the other end of Beckenham.

Some of the larger industries are listed below although there is not room to say much about them. Stanmar Products Ltd in Beckenham Road were dancing shoe manufacturers. J. Gardner & Co. Ltd, sheet metal and steel constructors, have now progressed to being thermal engineers and still trade from the Kent House

99 William Leslie Simons delivering milk from the Russell Farm dairy in 1908.

100   Holdstock's the confectioner and tobacconist was at 146 Croydon Road, Beckenham and this
picture was taken just before the First World War.

Lane industrial site. De Vere Ltd, industrial photographic apparatus manufacturers,
were at Thayers Farm Road for many years before moving out to New Addington.
Hooks Joinery Works started between the wars in Ravenscroft Road before moving
to Villiers where they are still operating. Smith & Haydn for many years had a
sweet factory at Elmers End as did Henry Flack's, the varnish manufacturers.
Sisley's the home-made sweet shop, was next to Sainsbury's. It was part of a small
chain store based in London.

   The list is endless and we regret having to omit so many. Look down all the
alley ways between shops as you pass them and you will be surprised at the
number of small businesses there are in the district. Before ending this chapter we
would like to mention the 'traders' we think of so nostalgically these days. The
cats' meat man with his tray of skewered pieces, the muffin man with his hand
bell, the 'stop me and buy one' Wall's ice cream man. Wall's had a factory in
Avenue Road and just round the corner in Ravenscroft Road was the Eldorado
depot. Besides deliveries of milk there were the travelling greengrocer and the
daily baker. Paraffin was delivered to the door to say nothing of the coal carts and
their patient horses. Last of all we should not forget the budding young entre-
preneurs who would earn pocket money by collecting the manure dropped by
these horses to sell for 2d. a bucket to local gardeners. Some of these youngsters
may well have gone on to start and run their own successful businesses.

Seven

Beckenham at Prayer

Church of England, Nonconformists, and Roman Catholic

In 1820 when the Langley property was put up for sale, Beckenham was described as a 'neighbourhood of the first respectability, and its situation particularly desirable for a nobleman or gentleman fond of hunting or shooting'. But was the situation equally delectable for the ploughman and cottagers upon the Beckenham land-owners' estates? Did the Church concern itself with their welfare? The old workhouse, for example (as we have seen in Chapter Three), was not a 'particularly desirable' residence for its 24 inmates.

In 1861 the population of the village was 2,391 and 30 years later it was 20,707. A soaring population meant expanding spiritual requirements, and this in turn was reflected by a mushrooming of places of worship. Beckenham had only needed one church in the village, the parish church of St George. The earliest known rector is William de Knapton in 1294 and a list of his successors up to the present day will

101 The old parish church of St George on the corner of Bromley Road and the High Street, *c*.1870. Its origins were probably in Saxon times and the building which served the needs of the small community until the late 19th century was based on a 14th-century structure.

91

102   The parish church of St George with an incomplete tower, *c.*1890. A choir vestry was added in 1890 but the tower remained uncompleted for the next 13 years, the bells being hung in a temporary wooden shed on the top of the unfinished tower during this period.

103   St George's parish church soon after completion in 1903. Externally it looks much the same today.

104 The lych gate of St George's dates back to the 13th century and is one of the oldest in the country. It was renovated in 1924 in memory of Stanley and Hedley Thornton who were killed in the First World War.

be found recorded just within the south door. In 1790 the old church was struck by lightning and partly destroyed by fire. It was 74 years before the main building was restored and enlarged. The present building only dates from 1885-7, during which period the old church was demolished and the new one erected without the services ever being interrupted. Its bell tower was not completed until 1903. The earliest records at St George's date from 1538 when it became compulsory for churches to keep records of all births, marriages and deaths in the parish. These records were stored in a vault in the churchyard during the Second World War as a protection against bomb damage, but they were badly attacked by damp.

As the Cator Estate developed it became necessary to have more space for the extra congregation and in 1864 St Paul's was built at New Beckenham.

The next church to be built was St Mary's, Shortlands, when the population for that area was only two hundred and sixty. Shortlands was formed as a separate parish in 1870. The original church was erected by the Wilkinson family of Shortlands House. The foundation stone for the present church was laid in 1953, and the new building consecrated two years later but the traditional lych gate was not replaced.

In 1870 work was also begun on the first vicarage, situated on ground partly occupied by the present church. This house, built by the local contractors, Syme & Duncan, was also damaged beyond repair by enemy action and subsequently demolished. The vicarage was the first dwelling to be completed by the then William Syme and John Duncan partnership. A parish room had been built close by Shortlands station in 1882 and this was later enlarged and went on to serve as the parish church after the bombing of 1940. The building was subsequently sold in 1966 when the new Church Hall was opened in St Mary's Avenue.

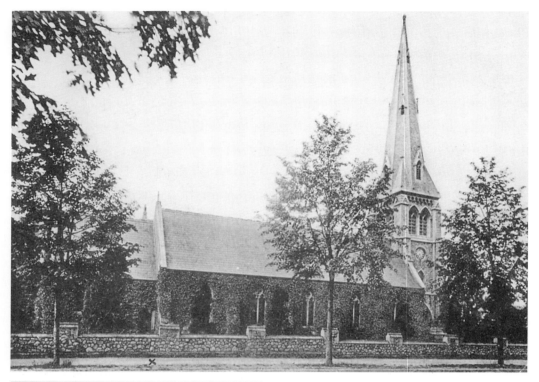

105 St Paul's Church at New Beckenham, *c.*1905. The first part of the church opened in 1864 and a separate parish was created when the main church, with pews for one thousand, was consecrated.

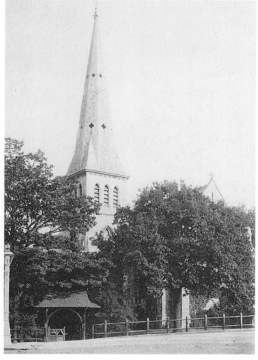

106 St Mary's, Shortlands. The church and fine lych gate were badly damaged by a landmine in 1940 and totally destroyed by a doodlebug four years later.

107 Over the years parish boundaries have changed many times but we show here the boundaries as they are today.

108 The Rev. Frederick Chalmers, Rector of Beckenham from 1851-73, was a good organiser. During his stay the steeple was repaired, a hot water heating system installed, the old fashioned square pews in the chancel and nave removed, the graveyard extended and the present stone wall erected in place of the old wooden palings.

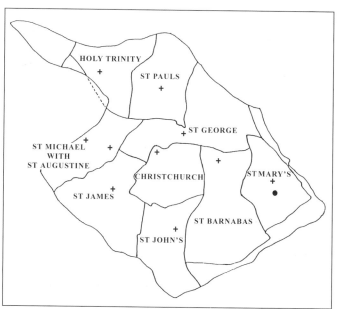

The last rector of St George's to preside over the undivided parish and a vestry which had the sole power over local affairs, both ecclesiastical and civil, was the Rev. Frederick Chalmers. He came to the parish in 1849, having previously had a very successful career as an officer in the Indian Army. With him came his father-in-law, Dr Marsh, also a clergyman and his sister-in-law Catherine who probably became even better known than the two men for her evangelistic activities and prowess as the author of several books. Between them they made a formidable team, preaching the gospel to the numerous navvies who had come to the area for building both the railways and the Crystal Palace.

In 1873, to help reduce the pressure on accommodation in the parish church, a small overflow corrugated iron chapel was erected in The Avenue and William Welch, a friend of the rector's, was invited to take charge. The new chapel was called Christ Church. William Welch was a staunch evangelical. He

wore a black Genevan gown and refused to wear a surplice until requested to do so by the Archbishop of Canterbury. Unfortunately, in the same year that he arrived Frederick Chalmers, who was then 68, decided to take up a quieter living at Nonington near Aylesham, where he died 12 years later. Albemarle Cator, the Lord of the Manor, nominated his brother William, an Oxford graduate and high church-man, to succeed to the living. It is difficult today to appreciate the strength of feeling which differences in doctrine aroused amongst churchgoers in Victorian times. In 1877 many policemen were required to quell a riot at a church and the clergyman concerned was tried and sentenced to imprisonment for his Anglo-Catholic practices. He and the man in whose house he was arrested now lie side by side in Elmers End Cemetery. Feelings also ran high in Beckenham, and as a result the congregation of Christ Church swelled from 45 to its capacity of 450 within a year.

When the Rev. William Cator came as rector to St George's he found a church closed except on Sundays, infrequent celebrations of the Holy Communion, Church doctrine of the lowest type, and Church life apparently almost dead. The simple worship to which the community had been accustomed was changed and, during the first part of 1874, 'ultra ritualistic and ultra sacramental novelties—including the confessional—were introduced' into the parish church. It became again a strong-hold of the Anglo-Catholic movement, causing serious divisions in the parish.

In order to meet the need for a larger place of worship than the tin hut in The Avenue, and also to provide for the wants of the large Evangelical section of the parish, Mr Cornelius Lea Wilson, known as the Squire of Beckenham, generously gave a site in 'The Fair Field' for the erection of a permanent church and vicarage, with schoolhouse, lecture hall and institute, together with a donation of £2,500 towards the Building Fund.

At first the new rector of Beckenham (the Rev. W. Cator) was very favourably disposed towards the erection of the new church, but before many months had passed his views underwent a complete change. The differences in doctrine and the realisation of the threat to his parish and income arising from the appearance of new and more splendid churches, built to serve the rapidly developing town, soured relations and from that time onward he persistently opposed every step connected with the establishment of the new church. However, the new scheme had advanced so far that his change of attitude did not affect the execution of the approved plans. The new Christ Church was consecrated by His Grace the Archbishop of Canterbury on 20 May 1876. The first incumbent was the Rev. William Welch, who had ministered in the temporary church in the Avenue. The old iron building was sold in 1877 and the money was used towards the debt on the lower school building. The church was severely damaged by a flying bomb during a raid in 1945 and not fully repaired until 1950.

There was for many years a chapel attached to Kelsey Manor called St Agatha's Chapel and in July 1871 the Annual Festival of the English Church Union was held there.

The parish of St Barnabas was formed in 1877 and a temporary building went up in Oakhill Road. The following year the building of the church was started. It

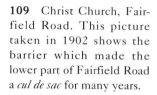

109 Christ Church, Fairfield Road. This picture taken in 1902 shows the barrier which made the lower part of Fairfield Road a *cul de sac* for many years.

was done in stages, the whole not being completed until 1933. Like many other churches, the building was badly damaged by bombs in 1944, but restored in 1948. In 1954 St Peter's Church Hall was built in Malmains Way to serve the Park Langley area and this has since been extended.

The building of Holy Trinity in Lennard Road in 1878 created another parish. The church was founded by Francis Peek, who was a tea merchant, and nephew of the founder of Peek, Frean and Company, the biscuit firm, and son of the founder of a tea firm called Peek Brothers. In 1876 his attention had been drawn to the growing needs of the poor neighbourhood which was springing up on the edges of the Cator Estate at Beckenham. Owing to some provision that the class of property must not be beneath a certain value on this estate, the work people crowded to the border, and there must have been about this time a population of several thousands at Penge. For some years the spiritual needs of these folk had been provided by a school-room service in Penge Lane, and it was here that Francis Peek saw his opportunity. He gained the sympathy of Albemarle Cator, who gave the site, part of a field adjoining the Alexandra Cottages. The first vicar was the Rev. S. Whitfield Daukes, who was then a curate at St Bartholomew's, Sydenham, and who married Mr Peek's eldest daughter, Lydia. The church was opened in 1878. The church house opposite was once an exclusive boys' school run by the Rev. Whitfield Daukes. This building was demolished and the site redeveloped as housing in the mid-1980s.

From 1868 until 1877 St Michael's church was a little tin hall in Harding's Lane, in the Alexandra district of Beckenham. When Holy Trinity, Lennard Road, was built, St Michael's moved to the Birkbeck Estate, and another hut was put up in Birkbeck Road in 1877, but it was not until 1898 that the building of the new church, which was to face Ravenscroft Road, was started and it was another 37 years before it was completed.

Until 1879 the little hamlet known as 'the Elmers End District' consisted of only a few hundred people. The area was served by a small iron church in the

110   St Michael's and All Angels on the Birkbeck Estate, *c*.1918. In 1908 the district was made a parish with Fr. Armstrong as the first vicar. St Michael's is very 'High Church' with incense, genuflecting, and confessionals.

Upper Elmers End Road opposite Goddard Road, but in February of that year a plot of land in Elmers End was given as a site for a church in a more accessible spot. By the end of that year the church was completed and the school was opened the following year. It was not until 1924 that St James' became a separate parish, the largest in Beckenham, and at that time, on the instruction of the Bishop of Rochester, the work, organisations and possessions associated with All Saints, Chaffinch Road, were transferred to St James. The Rev. C.J. Ritson who had been at All Saints took over the new parish of St James and remained there until his death in 1941. The church was badly damaged during the Second World War, but this did not stop any of the services, although the sermons were often somewhat short until full repairs could be made after the war was over. One of the authors (NT) recalls a war-time winter wedding there when everyone, including the bride and the vicar, had to wear top coats because there was no heating at all and the wind blew strongly through the broken windows.

1871 saw the erection of the Arthur Road Mission (now Churchfields Road). It was non sectarian, and evangelistic meetings were regularly held. Five years later the old Beckenham Mission was built in 1876 near Oakhill, Bromley Road. In 1937 the building was converted into flats and named 'Oakhill Court'.

With the continued growth in population the Nonconformist churches began to be established. Methodism began in the 1830s and, according to a Deptford Circuit Plan, services were held on Sundays. Methodist beginnings in Beckenham appear to be somewhat vague, but originally local preachers from Bromley held meetings in houses and the Public Hall was used for services. In the second half of the 19th century class distinctions were still clearly identifiable and many houses in Beckenham were very much 'upstairs - downstairs'. The rising middle classes, prospering in commerce and trade, were making their homes in this area. Broadly speaking, the 'top people' worshipped in established churches, whereas the non-conformist churches drew upon the new middle classes and their workers and people engaged in 'service'. Thus the scene was set for the birth of a new Wesleyan church in this developing area. Mr Tom Copeland, father of Rob Copeland the historian, recalled that in the late 1870s he could remember 'Cottage Meetings' being held in his father's house on Sunday evenings about once a month. The first Congregational services in Beckenham were started in 1877 by a group of people in an iron room at New Beckenham Station.

The foundation of Beckenham Congregational church in Crescent Road dates from 1878, when a small band of people, then known as 'Dissenters', decided to worship together. They met in what later became the Church Hall. This was destroyed by bombing in 1941 when the church keeper was killed, and rebuilt in 1950. Elmers End Free Church was an off shoot of Anerley Congregational Church, beginning as a mission in 1869. In 1872 an iron hut was erected in Eden Road and

111   Bromley Road Methodist Church, *c*.1907. The church on the corner of Bevington Road was not too badly damaged during the Second World War although it frequently lost windows and slates. The manse, however, was bombed and rendered uninhabitable. In the 1970s it was discovered that the spire was eroding and it was decided to remove it for safety.

112 Elm Road Baptist Church, *c.*1912. In the early days of its history part of the church was screened off because the congregation was not big enough to fill it. It escaped serious damage during the Second World War but suffered a fire in 1950.

five years later this was moved to Ancaster Road but later moved again to a freehold site in Langley Road. In 1884 a brick building was erected adjoining it, and this became the daughter church of Beckenham Congregational church. Shortly after 1900 it was made self supporting. An agreement was made that no other Free Church should be built in the area, which is why it is still called 'Free', although it is in fact affiliated to the Congregational Union. The present church in Goddard Road was opened in 1931—the two previous buildings being used as halls. By this time many more people had moved to the new estates in the Elmers End and Eden Park areas. The Congregational Church in Goddard Road was built in 1887.

Elm Road Baptist church was formally opened in 1883. It was built on the corner of Elm and Beckenham Roads before any of the houses were erected. The London Baptist Association at that time had a policy of building one new church each year. It is in this church that Enid Blyton was baptised.

St Augustine's Mission Hall, Churchfields Road (formerly Arthur Road) opened in 1886, and in 1910 a dual-purpose hall and church was started. This church was dedicated by the Bishop of Rochester on 1 July 1933 and consecrated on 31 May 1945. The Congregational church was started in Crescent Road, off Bromley Road and opened on 20 June 1888. In the same year a Wesleyan (Methodist) church was built in Bromley Road. The Mission Hall, known as the Lea Wilson Hall, stood in the High Street below Village Place until it was demolished in the 1920s when the High Street was widened. Another mission hall was built in Avenue Road, and the Ebenezer Baptist church at Elmers End near St Margaret's Villas in Croydon Road.

A mission hall had been built in Croydon Road, between the Cottage Hospital and Shaftesbury Road. This functioned under the auspices of Christ Church, and it was the worshippers from here who formed the nucleus of the congregation for the new church of St John the Baptist at Eden Park.

St John's is an Anglican church, with no incense, and the congregation worship simply. The Eden Park area had been in the parish of St James', Elmers End and during 1930 delicate but friendly negotiations had gone on. In an age when differences of churchmanship were a much more passionate issue than they have become today, there were strong feelings that there should be an evangelical presence in the developing areas of South Beckenham. St James' to the west and St Barnabas' to the east were there for those who preferred 'high' services. Something was needed for those who valued simplicity of worship and an emphasis on Bible teaching. The parish boundaries between Christ Church and St James' were redrawn and the new area became a separate parish of St John the Baptist, with an evangelical tradition.

The church was damaged several times during the war, losing windows and tiles, but it was not until just three months before the end of hostilities that it received its greatest blow. This was on 21 February 1945 when a V2 rocket landed causing grievous damage. The church itself lost all windows and half of the doors and the east wall was cracked away from the main structure. It was shored up temporarily but eventually had to be rebuilt. The organ loft was severely damaged and needed rebuilding and the vestries were virtually destroyed.

In 1907 two small churches were opened at Clock House. All Saints, which stood at the junction of Clock House Bridge and Chaffinch Road, was a Mission Church of St Augustine's and closed when St Augustine's was created as a separate parish. The other was the Wesleyan Chapel in Clock House Road. This had been built as The Beckenham High School in 1895 but the opening of The Beckenham Technical Institute killed off the High School. For a few years it became a not very successful dance-cum-vaudeville hall before being rented by the Wesleyans who finally bought it outright in 1909. The rooms used below ground by the Sunday school and for meetings of the Beckenham Photographic Society were once the theatre's dressing rooms.

The parish church was originally a Catholic church but from 1559, the year of the Reformation, until 1891 there was no Catholic parish or Catholic rector in Beckenham. The worship of the Catholic religion was ruthlessly suppressed by the State, in Beckenham and throughout England, and the celebration of Holy Mass was made a penal offence punishable by death. The old parish church of St George, therefore, fell into Protestant hands, and both it and its successor have been used for the worship of the Established Church ever since. Before the Reformation, Beckenham was in the Catholic Diocese of Rochester and Province of Canterbury, and had been so since Pope St Gregory the Great appointed St Augustine first Archbishop of Canterbury in AD 597, and St Justus first Bishop of Rochester. Far earlier than this England had been ruled by Catholic bishops in communion with the Holy See of Rome. On the restoration of the Catholic hierarchy in England in 1851, the Catholic prelates were forbidden by the State to resume their ancient titles, and Beckenham is now, therefore, in the Catholic diocese of Southwark and Province of Westminster. The Catholic parish of Beckenham was re-instated in 1891, and its first post-Reformation rector was the Right Rev. W.H. Kirwan, who later became Domestic Prelate to His Holiness the Pope.

By 1891 the first Roman Catholic church, the Church of the Transfiguration and St Benedict, was built in Overbury Avenue. The growth of Beckenham during the inter-war years made it increasingly necessary to have a more central place of worship, so in 1926 the church bought a hut in Village Way, which had formerly

113 Croydon Road Mission Hall. The iron hut of the Mission was transported to Eden Park Avenue and used for worship until the present St John's church was built in 1936.

114 St Edmund's Roman Catholic Church in Village Way, with the statue of the Virgin and Child by Jacob Epstein over the entrance.

been erected as a United Services Club by the YMCA in the First World War. The hut had become derelict so Father Pooley, the parish priest, and members of the congregation refurbished it to serve as a Catholic church, and this did yeoman service for many years. But the congregation was still growing and the hall became inadequate. In 1937 the foundation stone was laid for St Edmund's church—46 years after the Catholic mission was begun in Beckenham. Over the entrance is a carving of the Virgin and Child by Jacob Epstein, which, if the archbishop of the day had had his way, would have been replaced as being too modern. The church is architecturally interesting but its setting is marred by the adjoining multi-storey car park.

A small chapel stood for a few years in Beckenham Road between Birkbeck Road and Mackenzie Road on the site now occupied by Northam's shop in Beckenham Road. Two other churches complete the picture in Beckenham, the Evangelical church at The Hall in Cromwell Road, and the Christian Witness church in Rectory Road.

During the 19th and early 20th centuries many mothers would go to be 'churched' after the birth of a baby, and babies were not thought to thrive until they had been baptised. Youngsters were often confirmed when only 10 or 11 years old, if they were leaving home to find work or go into service. Customs have changed drastically since the Second World War.

Eight

Beckenham at Leisure

Sports and Pastimes

The earliest leisure activities enjoyed by the residents of Beckenham were naturally of a rural nature. Cricket was played by the villagers on the Fair Field and there were private cricket grounds both at Beckenham Place and Kelsey. The Fair Field took its name from an annual fair which was held there each August until the 1850s. It was not ideal for cricket as the level area was limited and the field was crossed by two footpaths. That was not perhaps as inconvenient as it would be today, for in those days there were no boundaries and sides did not have to declare. Sometimes the fielding side did not have an opportunity to bat before bad light forced them to retire. Horse-racing on the farm land between Croydon and Beckenham Roads was also a feature of the first half of the 19th century, until the Woodside racecourse opened over the Croydon boundary in 1866.

Organised sport dates from March 1866 when a group of enthusiasts led by Arthur Whaten of Beckenham Lodge met to found the Beckenham Cricket Club. They moved with remarkable speed; within two months they had leased the Beckenham Place ground at Foxgrove, which had been first laid out in 1835, held their first dinner at *The Three Tuns* with Peter Cator in the chair, and played their first match.

One of the main changes in recreation in Beckenham over the last few years is in the way sports are administered. For many years the council owned parks and recreation grounds, catering for a wide range of sports including bowls, cricket, five-a-side football, mini-soccer and rugby. The facilities were maintained by the council and the public and clubs were allowed to use then on payment of a fee which could be charged at an hourly rate, or the council could offer a season ticket which in the case of bowls would entitle you to play as many times as you liked from April to October.

Clubs were formed using these public facilities, some of them having been established for over 90 years. The clubs would ensure their members used the facilities in a responsible manner, and the council was happy to leave the actual organising of the sports in the hands of the club committees who would arrange the matches to be played.

In the early 1990s the government introduced Delegated Management and Bromley Council adopted this policy. This meant that the clubs had to accept much more responsibility in the running and maintenance of the council's facilities.

Up until then the council had employed staff to maintain the parks and recreation grounds; older readers will remember the park keeper with his peaked cap. Council-paid staff were responsible for cutting the grass, tending the flower beds and doing the 101 jobs throughout the year. Under Delegated Management the council was able to make all these workers redundant. Maintenance of the sporting facilities then became the responsibility of the clubs and the council employed outside contractors for the flower beds.

The first pilot scheme was tried out on the bowlers. There were 12 bowling greens within the Bromley area which included those in Beckenham. The bowling clubs held a meeting to discuss the position and arising from this an association was formed, the Bromley Council Bowling Clubs Association, abbreviated to the B.C.B.C.A., which all the clubs joined. Following this the council signed a 10-year agreement with each of the clubs. It became the responsibility of the B.C.B.C.A. to place the maintenance of the bowling greens, the shrubbery and pavilions with specialist contractors. Three prices had to be obtained for the work to a strict specification laid down by the council and the lowest quote was accepted. Bromley Council makes an annual cash grant to the B.C.B.C.A. to cover part of the maintenance costs and the clubs have to find the rest of the money themselves through their members' subscriptions and various fund-raising activities.

The B.C.B.C.A. are also responsible for repairing all damage caused by vandals to the greens and buildings and again are given an annual cash grant to cover this work. Beckenham is not alone in suffering from vandalism.

One unfortunate result of Delegated Management was that the park keeper was replaced with a security officer, who in his van visits all the parks in turn for a brief inspection. Apart from perhaps inevitable vandalism, Delegated Management has proved very successful and is now applied to all sporting activities on council property within the Bromley area.

Tennis was introduced in 1879 and two years later ladies were permitted to join. The sport became so popular that in 1886 an annual open tournament was introduced, which over the years has attracted many famous players to Beckenham. Once the week-long Lawn Tennis Tournament and Kent All-comers Championships served as a prelude to Wimbledon and drew an entry of international tennis stars to Beckenham every June. This unfortunately came to an end in 1996 due to a lack of sponsorship.

Two sports arenas were built at the Crystal Palace straddling the Penge/Beckenham boundary. Here were played the first Cup Finals and they became the scene of motor, motor bike and cycle racing. This complex was replaced by the National Sports Centre so, whilst the competitors involved came from all parts of the country, Beckenham can rightly feel that it has been and still is the scene of sporting endeavour from the most humble to that of the greatest national significance.

The town is also the home of the national sports grounds of three of the High Street banks and a number of other large commercial concerns. New Beckenham was the nearest place to the city where cheap flat land with a good train service was available. Unfortunately, reduced staff levels in banks and other businesses

115   Bowls in Beckenham Recreation Ground, *c*.1906. A game of bowls being played in the early days of the last century. A much larger jack (the white ball) was then used and the rink had a white line or tape down the centre.

116   The Tennis Club in Albemarle Road, *c*.1913. The club was the first to welcome competitors from the Soviet Union and the first to attract commercial sponsorship.

117 Foxgrove Cricket Pavilion. The club has continued to play on its original ground until the present day and includes Dr W.G. Grace among its famous visitors. The first county fixture—Kent *versus* Surrey—was played here in 1886.

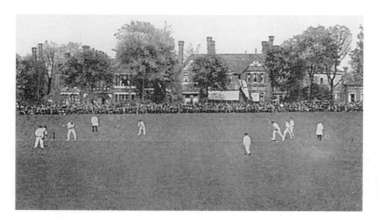

118 Cricket at the Crystal Palace. Foxgrove was by no means the only cricket ground in Beckenham. The London County Cricket Club, of which Dr W.G. Grace was Secretary and Manager from 1899 to 1908, had its home pitch in the grounds of Crystal Palace within the Beckenham boundary.

plus the increased interest in home entertainment, whether it be watching television or playing on the computer, has meant a great falling off in the number of people taking part in sports. This coupled with the lack of sports education in schools, has led to a generation for whom participation in active sport is no longer a part of life. In a competitive business world firms are no longer prepared to pay for the upkeep of facilities that are no longer required. The Lloyds Bank sports ground has been sold to the Kent County Cricket Club.

The Beckenham Men's Swimming Club was founded in 1879, but it did not have local facilities until the Baths were opened in 1901 on the site of the old Clock House. It had both covered and open air pools.

The original baths had no facilities for women bathers and the Ladies' Swimming Club was not formed until 1921. Beckenham swimmers have always been able to field strong teams in national and international competitions and several members of both clubs have represented Britain in the Olympics. The men's water polo team has been considered to be one of the finest in the country.

There was an ever-growing need to cater for schoolchildren once swimming became a compulsory school subject. However, it was 1938 before funds became available for the baths to be completely redesigned and up-dated. In the late 1990s the baths were demolished and replaced by an ultra-modern pool attached to the new leisure complex.

There were no public parks or recreation grounds and the loss of the Fair Field for a church and housing in the 1870s deprived the villagers of their traditional open space. Whilst Beckenham was surrounded by open fields this was not too much of a handicap. The rector frequently permitted his paddock in Rectory Road to be used for local sporting activities.

In 1890 the Local Board purchased a meadow in Croydon Road next to the Cottage Hospital for a recreation ground. It was formally opened the following year when the gentry, clergy, tradespeople and representatives of every organisation and all the schoolchildren, each wearing a medal specially minted for the occasion, made their way through the flag-bedecked village with bands playing and church bells ringing.

119 As can be seen in the picture, *c*.1928, the layout of the recreation ground has not greatly changed up to the present day. Hospital Meadow was added in 1914 and survived an attempted compulsory purchase for hospital extension in 1953. Access to the newly created Village Way took place in the 1930s.

120 The ornamental lake in Croydon Road Recreation Ground, *c.*1915. Its fountain, which came from the Clock House grounds, was replaced by the present paddling pool just before the war.

Alexandra Park was also opened in 1891, seemingly without ceremony. In 1907 a two-acre site belonging to the Churchfields Charity was purchased by the Council as a recreation ground for the Birkbeck area. A condition of the sale was that the name Churchfields Recreation Ground should be used to perpetuate the memory of its source.

The opening of the recreation grounds signalled an explosion of sporting activity. The annual cricket match between the coachmen and gardeners of the local gentry became an important annual event. Cricket was by no means the only sport popular in the area. Bowls at Croydon Road commenced as early as 1902 and the West Beckenham Bowling Club at the Alexandra ground was founded in 1919.

Football has always been popular, with many churches and schools fielding teams. The Beckenham & District League dates from 1912. Rugby has had a more chequered career. There was a Beckenham Rugby Club in 1876 but the present club commenced in 1894, though it was moribund from 1914 until 1924 and did not acquire its present site, a former polo ground, until a year or two later.

Beckenham has had four golf clubs, though only two still remain. The oldest, Beckenham Golf Club, opened in 1891, on the site of the former Woodside racecourse, and closed towards the end of the last war. The ladies formed their own club at Shortlands in 1894 to which men had only restricted access. In 1907 the Foxgrove Golf Club leased ground in Beckenham Place Park but lost its greens to the public in 1928, though the club house still remains. The last to be formed was Park Langley Club in 1910, the brainchild of the estate's developers.

121 Holy Trinity Church Football Team, 1905-6. Most schools and churches had their own enthusiastic football club. Apart from their long shorts, the kit is little different from today's wear.

122 Golf at Beckenham Place Park. Golf has been played in the park since 1907, first under the auspices of the Foxgrove Golf Club and since 1928 on a public course.

Angling was at one time allowed in the lake at Kelsey Park and for many years there has been a very active club using the small lake in the Crystal Palace grounds, whilst the lower boating lake is open to all for fishing.

Perhaps the biggest event to be staged was the annual flower show. The Alexandra estate tenants had formed the Alexandra District Floral and Horticultural Society in 1868 and held annual shows from that date. At their first event over 300 money and special prizes were awarded. Beckenham Horticultural Society was formed in 1892 and proceeded to mount annual shows which rivalled Chelsea. There were dozens of large gardens in the town each with extensive glass houses run by several gardeners. The incentive to outdo your neighbour was intense and the resulting spectacle something we shall never see again. Support dwindled as gardens became smaller and the horticultural society finally collapsed in the 1970s, leaving only its floral art section to continue as a separate organisation.

In addition to the annual flower show, Croydon Road Recreation Ground has been the scene of almost every civic and national occasion the town has celebrated. The shallow oval depression near the entrance, sometimes referred to as the Hippodrome, was flooded in winter and used as a skating rink. The same site was the scene of a unique occasion in 1902 when, to celebrate the coronation of King Edward VII, Britain's first manned mail-carrying balloon soared aloft with M. Gaudron, a French balloonist and Dr Barton, a local medical practitioner, as crew.

123   Crystal Palace Angling Club's Pavilion, *c*.1959. Sadly, the pavilion was burnt down some years ago by vandals.

124 Beckenham Flower Show, 1905. Support started to dwindle after the First World War and the Society finally collapsed in the 1970s though its Floral Art Section has survived to this day as a separate organisation.

Mail was dropped at three points in Kent and the balloon itself then crossed the Channel and landed near Calais. Two more balloons ascended from the same spot at the 1905 flower show and, although by this time airmail had lost its novelty, the few cards which have survived are eagerly sought by collectors.

Although the annual Flower Show and the Hospital Fete together with its traditional fair are no longer held, the crowning of the Beckenham May Queen still takes place on the first Saturday in April every year, following a procession through the district of all the May Queens and their attendants from West Wickham, Eden Park, Penge, Anerley, and Hayes.

Perhaps the proudest occasion the recreation ground was to witness was in 1935 when the Lord Mayor of London drove into the park in his ceremonial coach to present a Charter of Incorporation as a Borough on behalf of H.M. The King.

A proposal to purchase the whole of the Manor estate for the town was rejected but fortunately a later one to acquire the Kelsey grounds was successful. It had been realised that there was a need for an ornamental park as distinct from a recreation ground. Kelsey Manor was demolished in 1921, the site sold for housing and the proceeds used to improve access and acquire the extension fronting onto Wickham Road which was opened in 1936.

Between the wars the town pursued a generous policy of acquiring additional recreational space for its residents. Cator Park, formerly a private park called the

125   Thornton's Shop decorated for the Coronation in 1902. Three hundred cards were overprinted 'BECKENHAM CELEBRATION. Despatched from the Clouds by Balloon Post, Coronation Day, Aug. 9th 1902'. The cards were sold for 3d. each and were to be addressed and stamped, with a written message if desired, and then left at Thornton's library. The cards were quickly sold out.

126   *Below left*. Front of a Balloon Card. Today only about half a dozen of the 1902 Coronation Balloon cards are known to exist. Airmail collectors covet them because they were the first mail in Britain to be flown in a manned balloon. At an auction in 1980 one of these cards fetched £1,500.

127   *Below right*. Back of a Balloon Card. The postmark on this card is 'Dover, 4 November 1902'. The delay was due to the fact that one of the sacks of mail landed in a field and was undiscovered for three months.

Kent House Pleasure Ground, was acquired, as were the Stanhope playing fields. The site of Eden Farm was bought by the local council early this century when the house was demolished and later Crease Park, facing on to Village Way, was created and named after Alderman James Crease, who was the second Charter Mayor and one of the five freemen of the Borough.

The schoolchildren had not been forgotten and in 1928 the Elgood playing fields were opened between Village Way and Manor Way. The local elementary schoolchildren of all ages walked there for their weekly games and for the annual inter-school sports which were one of the highlights of the scholastic year. Another equally important event was the inter-school gala when the first-class baths rang with the deafening roars of encouragement from the gallery and water-side.

Whilst catering for a wide range of sporting activities, Beckenham at first lacked public facilities for cultural interests. In 1882 a Public Hall Co. was formed to purchase part of the site of the old manor house from the Local Board and build and operate a hall on the site. Opening in 1884, it was immediately in great demand. Most of the ground floor was leased to a gentlemen's club which still exists in part of the building almost unchanged to this day. The public hall still largely retains its original appearance. It remained the property of the private company until after the war when it was purchased by Beckenham Council.

128 Fishing for tiddlers in Cator Park. Youngsters have always enjoyed 'tiddler fishing' although, now the local streams have been culverted to reduce flooding, there are few places left for them to be able to enjoy this simple pleasure.

129 Elgood Playing Fields: a march past and salute at the opening of Elgood Playing Fields in 1928. Hitler had not yet come to power and the raised arm salute did not have its later significance.

In 1897 Church House was opened in the gardens of the old rectory fronting on to the High Street. This was much used by church organisations and other societies. The Photographic and Cine Societies were both founded in its committee rooms and the horticultural society used it not only to hold meetings but also to house its considerable library of over 500 volumes. Before the advent of wireless and television people had to arrange their own entertainment and clubs and societies of every sort were well supported. The founding in 1883 of a College of

Music and Art in Rectory Road which advertised a staff of no less than 50 professors, and the opening of the public hall the following year, sparked off a flurry of musical activity. The Beckenham Orchestral Society was founded in 1883, the Choral Society in 1885, and the Amateur Dramatic Society five years later. Round about 1890 the Beckenham Brass Band was formed and practised at the *George*, which was also the home of an indoor bowls club. The outbreak of war sounded the death knell for most of these organisations for, just as today, they depended in large measure on the efforts and enthusiasm of relatively few individuals, many of whom did not return from the fighting. Between the wars some societies, such as the Amateur Dramatic Society, reformed. A Beckenham Society, the forerunner of the present Civic Society, also made its appearance between the wars.

This was also the hey day of the picture palace. Beckenham's first cinema, 'The Pavilion', opened in October 1914 with a programme of patriotic war films

130   The 'Pavilion' cinema on the corner of Village Way, in the 1920s. There are still people in Beckenham who can recall the old silent films, the tinkling piano and the lady who threaded your token on a string when you entered. Even the new-fangled tip-up seats were a great novelty and sometimes a snare to the uninitiated.

131 The 'Odeon' cinema
at Elmers End in the 1950s.
This cinema opened just as
the Second World War
commenced but only
survived for 18 years before
competition from tele-
vision took its toll.

and all proceeds were donated to the town's war relief fund. It did not long survive
the 'Regal' which opened in 1930 and is still with us today as the 'ABC' recently
renamed the 'Odeon'. Typically, it provided an escape from humdrum reality with
fitted carpets, soft lighting and luxurious fittings not yet standard in the average
home. Before the film started the lights would dim and the organist would slowly
rise from the pit, playing his mighty Wurlitzer ablaze with light. The 'Regal'
cinema had a seating capacity of 1,980 and opened on 22 September 1930 with
'The Rogue Song'. The 'Odeon' at Elmers End opened on 26 August 1939 with
'The Man In The Iron Mask'. It had a seating capacity of 1,518 but, due to the
popularity of television in the 1950s, it closed in January 1957 when the site was
redeveloped as an office complex, now the headquarters of the international
engineering firm of Maunsell Ltd. Its last screening was 'Dance With Me Henry'
and 'Overland Pacific'.

A public library, opened in 1939, was one amenity Beckenham was surprisingly
late in acquiring. Subscription libraries were run by Boot's, Smith's and Thornton's,
so the Council presumably felt this was adequate until the development of the
estates in the town centre and along Croydon Road.

Nine

Beckenham at War

1914-1918 and 1939-1945

Beckenham has never been found wanting in times of war. On 22 April 1798, 63 residents gathered on the Fair Field and resolved to form an 'Armed Association' to defend the country against the French under Napoleon should the need arise, but their services were not required. In the second half of the 19th century military cadets were a commonplace sight in the town. The East India Company's Military Training College was situated at nearby Addiscombe and its trainees were encouraged to visit the town by Frederick Chalmers, rector of Beckenham from 1850 to 1873, himself an ex-Indian Army man. In 1900, during the Boer War, a Volunteer Corps was formed and had its headquarters at Elm Cottage in the High Street.

Not everyone considered that it was patriotic to give up one's job to serve the country. One volunteer, returning after fighting in the Boer War, was given a reference which read: 'This young man had so little consideration for his employer and his own prospects that he abandoned his job to fight in South Africa'.

The 1914-18 War had a drastic effect on the town. The cream of its manhood enrolled in the armed forces, many of them never to return. A number of the larger buildings became military headquarters or hospitals to take care of the wounded. Christ Church Halls and Balgowan Schools, for example, became military hospitals, the former only until 1916 when the operation was moved to the newly-built Lennard Road Girls County School. This 130-bed establishment had an operating theatre, X-Ray and the latest electrical apparatus. It closed on the last day of 1918.

Throughout the county Red Cross detachments, St John's Ambulance Brigade and Territorial forces had been preparing since 1912 in case of emergency. The Beckenham Red Cross had been doing their training at the Cottage Hospital over the previous two years. Kent 86 Red Cross detachment took over the hasty preparation of the Christ Church Halls and converted the rooms into a hospital of 50 beds. Kent 96 detachment, aided by Kent 162, at first assisted Kent 86 at the Christ Church Schools site but they were then transferred to the new school building in Balgowan Road. Like Lennard Road, this was fully equipped with the latest technology and had 100 beds to start with, but the addition of two marquees enabled the accommodation to be increased to 240 beds. The hospital closed on 31 March 1919 and both schools were shortly afterwards returned to the Education Board.

132   Christ Church Hospital in 1915. This Red Cross hospital, together with the annexe at Kelsey Cottage, was closed and transferred to the new building in Lennard Road in 1916 but the name Christ Church Hospital was retained.

133   Balgowan School Military Hospital in Balgowan Road, *c*.1917. The hospital admitted 5,257 soldiers and a further very large number attended as out-patients.

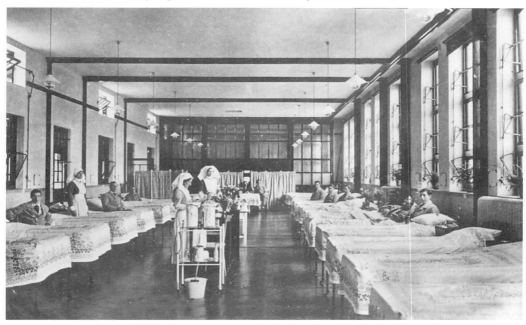

134 Funeral of a Belgian soldier in Fairfield Road in 1915. Many of the casualties did not survive and, like this Belgian soldier, were buried with full military honours at Elmers End cemetery.

When one considers the vast numbers treated at these two hospitals alone, it brings home to us how many thousand personnel were injured during the First World War, to say nothing about the numbers who did not survive to be sent home. Beckenham is the only place we are recording here, but it must be appreciated that numerous other towns in the country can tell the same tale. Two thousand wounded arrived at Bromley South station on the first day that casualties were returned to Britain.

Besides the wounded personnel the village was host for several battalions of soldiers—English, Scottish, Irish and Canadian who were billeted throughout the district wherever anyone had a spare bed. Men in khaki were an all too familiar sight and so were those in hospital blue. Beckenham also became home for many Belgian refugees within a month of the commencement of hostilities, whose children went to Bromley Road school. In a matter of weeks village life changed drastically, never to return quite the same after the armistice. The first Belgians to arrive were 36 trades people who had lost their all and been compelled to leave their country. Two large houses, one at the junction of Manor Road and Wickham Road, and one at Shortlands, were equipped with all the necessary furniture and bedding. Two more houses and a clothing depot were quickly organised.

135 Oakwood, Shortlands, seen here in 1915, was taken over by one of the military transport divisions.

136 The Y.M.C.A. Canteen, *c.*1917. To satisfy the social needs of the military visitors the Y.M.C.A. erected a large hut as a services club in the *cul-de-sac* (later to become Village Way) by the side of the 'Pavilion' cinema, on the site of the future St Edmund's Hall.

137 Beckenham's Peace Parade in 1919. Everyone turned out to celebrate and enjoy the Peace Parade as it wound its way from the parish church through the High Street. Every organisation which had been connected with the war effort took part.

Many of the large buildings affected by their military occupation were never again to be family homes and were eventually demolished. When peace came Beckenham was a very different place. Between the wars the memory of the carnage remained vivid among those who survived. One in 10 of our men died. 11 November, Armistice Day, with its two minutes' silence was solemnly observed each year. Memorials were erected in prominent positions at the end of the High Street and outside St Mary's Shortlands. A new extension was added to the Cottage Hospital in memory of those who gave their lives. The lych gate outside St George's parish church was restored in memory of Hedley and Stanley Thornton, two of the sons of the town's newspaper proprietor who were killed in the conflict. The British Legion had a strong local following, with headquarters first in the Y.M.C.A. hut and later in the Manor House in the High Street.

138   Like so many of the large houses in Beckenham, Village Place in the High Street became a military establishment for the duration of the war.

139   War memorials of all sizes were erected in every town and village throughout Britain. This one, seen here in the 1920s, was near St Mary's church at Shortlands.

The 1939-45 war was to have a very different but equally drastic and more direct effect on the town. Parks, sports grounds and other open sites were dug up for allotments often sharing the space with soldiers, anti-aircraft guns and barrage balloons. There was even a rail-mounted gun which was shunted out from its tunnel hideout on the Sanderstead line from time to time. Every able-bodied person not conscripted into the forces was involved in the war effort in one way or another. A.R.P. personnel, both male and female, were recruited for firewatching and other necessary duties, such as a census on the size of water tanks in houses which might be needed in an emergency. An Auxiliary Fire Service was recruited and the Local Defence Volunteers, later named the Home Guard, absorbed not only the older men but also youngsters awaiting conscription into the armed forces. Initially only a few rifles were issued to the staff in the factories at Elmers End and at the Borough Electricity Works but, as in the early part of the war there was a very real threat of an attack on London by German ground forces, detailed plans were drawn up for the defence of the Borough and the Capital in which the 1,000-strong 55th West Kent Battalion of the Home Guard had a key role to play. So important was this role considered to be that the local battalion was personally inspected by no less a person than H.M. The King soon after its formation.

140 Only two decades after the signing of the Armistice, it was necessary once again to prepare for a further conflict. This 1941 photograph shows the newly formed Home Guard being inspected in Beckenham Recreation Ground.

At the start of the Second World War the whole country was plunged into darkness; all street lighting was switched off and windows were 'blacked out'. People very quickly adapted to managing with torch light. However, it was slightly different in the First World War. The Urban District Council were quickly asking 'Is Beckenham Too Dark?'—and this when the street lighting was at first only reduced. It was then suggested that they be suppressed completely but it was felt that in certain places this would be dangerous, such as the path under the railway at the Kingshall Road allotments. There were no really hard and fast rules about a blackout at first, and at the council meeting in mid-October 1918 it was reported that the Beckenham end of Venner Road was in darkness, but at the Sydenham end the lights were brighter than they had ever been. Also, whilst Beckenham was in darkness, the Crystal Palace was a blaze of lights and could be seen for miles. Doubtless everywhere conformed to the regulations once the Zeppelin raids commenced.

Days before the Second World War actually started many thousands of school-children and mothers with young children were evacuated from large towns into more rural areas where it was felt they would be safer from air attacks. Many left on private schemes for Canada and the U.S.A. Beckenham did not really organise evacuation until the raids became so severe during the winter of 1940-41, and even then children had to live on the Penge side of the Clock House railway line. Thus if you lived in Sidney Road you were considered to be at risk but safe the other side of the railway in Clock House Road. However, the whole area was soon to be at risk as raids intensified and the flying bombs and later the rockets arrived.

A few evacuees never returned to Beckenham, preferring their new life in the country, and many kept in touch with their foster families for many years. A small group of 21 girls left Lennard Road school early one dark and dismal morning in January 1941 and with their teacher spent the next 16 months in Exeter before several of them were bombed in the Exeter blitz of April 1942. One girl lost her life in a bombing incident in Penge when she returned home, but of the rest half of them are still in touch with each other after 60 years and now have an annual reunion with Miss Rabson, who was their teacher in exile.

Schools were late opening for the autumn term 1939. Some forms only attended mornings or afternoons whilst other were taught in local houses. As the war progressed lessons often had to continue in the shelters but education, although interrupted for many, had to and did continue much as before. Allotments became highly desirable as food convoys were attacked by submarines. School playing fields and park land were dug up to provide more growing space. Girls at 18 years of age who did not want to join the armed services were able to go into the Land Army and help 'Dig for Britain', whilst the boys could opt to become Bevin Boys and go down the coal mines. For some years after the war boys were still being called up at 18 years of age to do a two-year National Service stint.

Ration books and gas masks were everyday articles. One never went out at the beginning of the Second World War without carrying a gas mask in its little card-board box. But as time went on these were left at home more and more often. Clothing coupons caused everyone to 'make do and mend' and an old parachute

141   The funeral cortège of 19 Auxiliary Fire Service personnel killed in a blitz on the East End in April 1943.

was highly prized for making 'undies'. Wallpaper disappeared and rooms, when needing to be redecorated, were painted with distemper. Some people turned vegetarian in order to get an increased cheese ration and many started to keep chickens in their back gardens to help out with the egg supplies. Pig Clubs sprang up everywhere and nothing was allowed to be wasted. How things have changed since those days!

Beckenham was a legitimate target for air attack; not only did it lie on a main rail line to the capital, it also housed a large electronics factory as well as several smaller ones—even the Chinese Garage was on war work. It was also a convenient place to drop a bomb-load should an aircraft be frustrated in reaching the centre of London. During the war nearly 1,000 high explosive bombs, 10,000 incendiaries and 79 V1/V2 rockets rained down on the Borough, killing 360 people and injuring almost 1,800 more.

142 Spitfire Fund Raising at Muirheads in 1940. The Mayor of Beckenham poses in front of an aircraft to publicise the event.

Lord Stamp, Charter Mayor of Beckenham, was an early victim when his Shortlands home received a direct hit in April 1941. Two days later 21 Beckenham firemen perished in an incident whilst on duty in the East End. The most conspicuous damage resulted from flying bomb attacks in July 1944 in which the Albemarle Road area and St Mary's church, Shortlands were both hit twice and Elmers End bus garage was totally destroyed. The worst loss of life came at the beginning of the following month when a crowded café in Beckenham Road was hit. In January 1945, just when everyone was beginning to think the worst was over, a V1 wrecked Christ Church and the surrounding houses. This was the 73rd and last flying bomb to fall on the town, killing 12 people and seriously injuring several others. Although the church was extremely damaged, it was possible a few months later to hold a V.E. Day thanksgiving service amid the ruins.

Many awards for bravery were won during the wars both by military personnel and civilians. We mentioned in Chapter V Lt. John Norwood who earned the V.C. at Ladysmith. William Evans (Manchester Regt.) won the Victoria Cross at Guillemont, France in 1916. He was buried at Elmers End cemetery in 1937. Two more V.C.s connected with Beckenham were awarded during the Second World War. L/Cpl J.P. Harman (Royal West Kent Regt.) won his V.C. in April 1944 when the Japanese in Burma attempted to invade India. Lance Corporal John Harman was born in Beckenham and his medal was awarded posthumously. Captain

143 In one of the worst incidents in the borough, both sides of this area of Beckenham Road were devastated when a V1 hit Bill Trendall's crowded café at lunchtime on 2 August 1944, killing 44 people.

144 St George's parish church was extensively damaged in July 1944 when two flying bombs devastated the area. The nearby shops and houses were never rebuilt and the resultant open space is today a pleasant oasis.

145 Incendiaries at St Michael's church. Sadly, within ten years of being finished St Michael's and All Angels was completely destroyed by fire during an air raid on 24 March 1944 but was rebuilt and consecrated on 7 October 1956.

146 A wedding in St Michael's church hall. Whilst the church was being rebuilt all services were conducted in the church hall and in the case of weddings most photographs were taken in the vicarage grounds. This wedding was on 29 April 1950.

P.J. Gardner (Royal Tank Regt.) received the Victoria Cross for his bravery during an attack by German tanks at Tobruk in November 1941. He had earlier received the M.C. Capt. Gardner was Chairman and Managing Director of J. Gardner & Co. Ltd, the steel fabrication company who built their factory on the site of the old Beckenham brick works.

Despite all this trauma and tragedy, a semblance of normal life went on both for the residents and their numerous military guests. Regular dances were held at the 'Regal' and astronomical quantities of cups of tea and buns were consumed within the Christ Church Halls. British Restaurants were also a regular feature of life at the St George's Church Hall in the High Street and at Muirheads. A Prisoner-of-War Camp 'Summerhouse No. 233' was situated in Beckenham Place Park and when peace came the prisoners helped to build the council houses in Beck Lane, near the Elmers End bus garage. Many American and Canadian troops were stationed around the area and some married local girls and took them home as G.I. brides.

During the Second World War there was a campaign to encourage everyone to have holidays at home, and an outdoor stage was erected in the Croydon Road recreation ground on which entertainments were staged during the summer months. This action had not been necessary in the First World War as the majority of people then could not afford to go away on holiday.

Nearly a hundred and fifty years had lapsed between the villagers gathering in the Fair Field with their weapons and their descendants gathering in shelters to escape the devastation of pilotless aircraft. Truly Beckenham can be said to have experienced war in many of its aspects.

Ten

Post-War Beckenham

1945 to the Present Day

The years since the last war have witnessed change in Beckenham almost as radical as that which converted the original village into a town. Virtually every vestige of local control has passed either to regional or national authorities and Beckenham is now a dormitory suburb. This change did not come all at once and was due to a variety of reasons. Hospitals and electricity supply passed into outside hands due to political decisions made soon after war ended. Beckenham hospital at first benefited from the change with improved facilities but in recent years its future role has become uncertain. Its position was not helped by competition from the 30-bed Sloane Private Hospital which opened in Albemarle Road in 1980 and has since almost doubled in size. Control of the fire service was lost at the beginning of the war when it was realised that a vast increase in resources and a standardisation of equipment was essential to meet the threat posed by air attack. The fire station next to the public hall became redundant when a new combined fire and ambulance station was opened by the London Fire Brigade in Beckenham Road in 1986. The final blow, as far as Beckenham is concerned, came in 1965 when the Borough was abolished and became part of a new London administrative unit called, rather confusingly, the London Borough of Bromley.

Perhaps the most drastic change to take place in the area stemmed from the loss of corporate identity and the gradual concentration of local government functions in Bromley once the Borough had been abolished. The Town Hall stood derelict for a considerable time before being replaced by a Marks & Spencer food store in 1992. Fortunately its foundation stone, and that of the 18th-century rectory which had also stood on the site, were preserved and can now be seen in the parish church across the road.

The ambitious North Central Beckenham Redevelopment Scheme envisaged the complete replacement of the remaining shops and houses by an open space surrounded by modern office buildings. Bromley Road School was to be demolished as were the buildings on the corner of Rectory Road, the latter being replaced by a triumphal arch leading into the town hall complex. The scheme only partially succeeded inasmuch as Church Road was closed and Albemarle Road re-aligned to form the first stage of a proposed bypass for the town centre, thus creating the existing 'Beckenham Green'. The Church was more than willing to fit in with the council's plans, as even before the war it had regarded Church House as unsuited

147   The 1963-4 Council gathered in the Council Chamber for a formal photograph.

148   The old Council Hall, headquarters of Beckenham Council and its predecessors from 1882 to 1932 being demolished to make way for commercial redevelopment.

149   Beckenham Green. This small, peaceful area has been created out of the havoc caused by two flying bombs which fell behind the church in 1944.

to modern requirements and something of a liability because of its state of repair. As a result, the church acquired the site of the old main Post Office in Albemarle Road on which to build a new hall, and Church House was demolished to be replaced by the present St Bride's House. The bypass proposal was not proceeded with and this, together with the massive increase in traffic, has contributed to the decline of the High Street. Beckenham is in an area with one of the highest levels of car ownership in the country. It is nothing unusual to see front gardens being used as parking space for two or even three cars. Car parking is yet another problem, particularly near the stations, where commuters leave their cars all day, thereby frustrating the short-term visitor. Until recently all new buildings had to have generous parking space but there are now proposals, aimed at reducing car use, to lower these standards, particularly in areas such as Beckenham which has good public transport.

The nearby railway station has survived largely unchanged, though suburban trains are now interspersed with long sleek Eurostar trains on their way to and from Brussels and Paris. Its surroundings have, however, changed radically. The forecourt has undergone its fourth transformation from nursery garden, 1930s shopping parade, timber yard and now into the Tramlink terminus. The goods yard to the rear, which within living memory received cattle on the hoof destined for local butchers, is now a Waitrose supermarket.

It is the High Street itself which has undergone the most profound transformation due to the change from town to dormitory suburb. Many present-day Beckenham residents are working, own at least one car, and do their shopping in the evening or at weekends which now includes a Sunday. As a result, gone are most of the national chains of shops such as MacFisheries, Montague Burton, International Stores, Home and Colonial and most recently Safeway, Iceland and Tandy. Only Marks & Spencer and Sainsbury's have so far defied this trend. The

150 The Centenary of the Railway in 1956 was commemorated by a steam-hauled excursion which is seen here leaving Beckenham Junction.

remaining relatively small retailers in the traffic-choked High Street, under increasing pressure from high rates and rents set by outside bodies, find it difficult to compete with the nearby supermarkets with their longer opening hours, free parking, weather protection and ever expanding range of goods and services. They are being gradually replaced by restaurants, public houses, charity shops and estate agents more attuned to the needs of the changed population; the two former benefit particularly from the lighter evening traffic and relaxed parking restrictions. It is now true to say that Beckenham town centre really only comes to life in the evenings. The 'Regal' cinema, now called the 'Odeon', looks largely unchanged from the outside. It was, however, split into three smaller screens with the loss of its organ and has now been divided still further into six screens.

It is not only the shopping streets which have undergone a transformation since the war. At the end of hostilities virtually the whole of the Cator Estate, including such much-used thoroughfares as Albemarle Road, was served by unmade roads of the sort still found at the top end of The Avenue and elsewhere. The Knoll, Plawsfield Road and Barnmead Road are still unmade for their entire length and the latter has been made a private road with restricted access. Not only have these roads been made up and their maintenance passed to the Council, but many large Victorian and Edwardian houses were demolished to make way for blocks of flats or small town houses. Bomb sites were rebuilt as office blocks, several of which have never been fully occupied such as the ones on Beckenham Road at Mackenzie Road and Thayers Farm Road. Developments were not confined to the

151   This early Tesco's supermarket is seen in 1968 during one of the periodic floods which used to affect this part of Beckenham whenever there was exceptionally heavy rain.

152   The interior of Beckenham's original Sainsbury's when it converted to self-service in 1963.

Cator Estate; the value of land in the area had become so high that every piece of undeveloped land was sought after by developers. In an imaginative deal the Council traded land for housing at the rear of the swimming baths for a new leisure centre.

A limited number of special lace panels was made by Dobsons and M. Browne & Co. Ltd of Nottingham. They were presented to Sir Winston Churchill, the Air Council, the Royal Air Forces Association, the City of London and to a limited number of towns including Beckenham, Croydon and Sheerness. These lace panels are 15 feet high and ornately designed with scenes commemorating the war. The Beckenham panel was loaned to Royal Air Force Station Biggin Hill in 1970 for safekeeping and was displayed in the Officers' Mess. With the closure of the Station in 1992 the lace was transferred to Bromley where, after refurbishment, it has been hung in the Civic Centre for all to see. Other mementoes of Beckenham's history are now stored in a museum in distant Orpington.

By 1951 Beckenham had a population of 75,000 (10,000 more than Bromley), making it one of the largest towns in Kent. Local newspapers had for many years relied on the durability of old-fashioned equipment and the loyalty and enthusiasm of their founding families for their continued existence. Individually they did not generate the sort of profits required to invest in new technology and as the years went by they became increasingly vulnerable to take-over by larger, better equipped organisations. Thus in 1955 control of the *Beckenham Journal* was sold to the *Kentish Times* who retained Victor Thornton as editor until his death in 1966, but immediately closed the local printing works and transferred production to Sidcup. Since that

153 The Beckenham Lace. The lace depicts badges and national flowers of the allied Air Forces, views of London, and various British and German aircraft.

date increasing commercial pressures have forced the closure of the local office and, whilst the name is still mentioned in the heading, the Beckenham content is often small. The rival *Beckenham & Penge Advertiser* has fared little better, also closing its local office and quite recently abandoning the use of the title altogether. Their future has been made more precarious by the appearance in 1965 of free newspapers funded entirely by advertising.

The loss of a local newspaper with its crusading editor, imbued with local patriotism, is yet another factor contributing to the decline of the town's identity. Editor Victor Thornton joined others to persuade the Council to close the High Street in order that a fair could be held to celebrate the Queen's coronation in 1953. And it was Victor Thornton who made his own contribution to the day by producing an open-air performance of *The Merry Wives of Windsor* in a replica Elizabethan playhouse beside the big tulip tree in Kelsey Park. It was thanks to Victor's father, Tom Thornton, that Kelsey Park was available for this performance. Tom had fought hard to convince the Council that the Kelsey Estate should be bought for use as a public park and it was due to his efforts that this was done and the park opened in 1913. Plans had already been drawn up to turn the estate into a housing complex when the Council stepped in to buy it.

As happened after the First World War, many societies which suspended their activities in 1939 did not revive after the war. One which did survive was the Beckenham Amateur Dramatic Society, founded in 1923 by the renowned professional actor Martin Lewis. Another post-war theatrical venture of note is the Beckenham Little Theatre. It started life in 1948 as a play-reading session in the children's section of Beckenham Library, graduated to actual performances and for a spell leased the H.J. Harvey Memorial Hall. Thanks to the generosity of the builders, Syme and Duncan, and the enthusiasm of Victor Thornton and others, it now has its own 47-seat theatre, a converted private house which opened in 1960 at the corner of Manor Road and Bromley Road. It was until recently unique in presenting adult plays performed entirely by children. Children grow up and they provide the recruits for the more senior sections of the theatre. Many present-day professionals owe their initial training to this modest theatre.

A vacant allotment site at Kangley Bridge was used for industrial and warehousing units hoping to provide employment for the local population. The general trend, however, is for industry to leave Beckenham. The Muirhead/Twinlock complex has been replaced by a Tesco supermarket. More recently, due to a series of take-overs, the famous Wellcome name has disappeared from the scene, leaving only a minor part of the new Glaxo Smith Kline company. The Victorian mansion with its former 'chapel' has been converted into apartments whilst the bulk of the site is now a housing estate whose cramped layout contrasts dramatically with

154 The scene on the stage as (the late) Dick Emery declares the theatre open in the presence of the Mayor and Mayoress of Beckenham, 24 September 1960. Victor Thornton can be seen sitting at the right of the picture.

155 None of the participants on the stage in Victor Thornton's production of Shaw's masterpiece 'Pygmalion' was over 15 years old. This show was performed at the Beckenham Baths in 1949.

neighbouring more spacious Park Langley. Some industry and commerce still survives, notably Bolloms paint factory and Maunsells Engineering headquarters at Elmers End, whilst at Clock House the Independent Registrars has recently been joined by the regional headquarters of NHS Direct.

Educational changes are still continuing, such as opting out and the new assessment procedures at seven and 14 years of age. Highfield Primary School and Clare House Primary School, the latter built on the same site as a former private school of the same name, have been built in the Shortlands district and Worsley Bridge opened in 1953 to take the Junior Mixed pupils from the overcrowded Bromley Road School. Woodbrook School in Hayne Road opened in 1970 on the site of a private school of the same name and, like its predecessor, caters for children with special needs. The Beckenham Convent school for girls in Foxgrove Road closed in 1988 owing to its inability to recruit staff and, as so often happens, its buildings have been demolished and replaced by a close of modern houses. Langley Park School for Boys and Langley Park School for Girls have both opted out of the state system as also has Kelsey Park School for Boys.

The lodges at the entrance to the Beckenham Place estate in Southend Road have been made listed buildings as also have three of the original large Victorian houses at the eastern end of Beckenham Place Park Road. These are set amongst dense trees some of which are the subject of a Tree Preservation order. A number of conservation areas have been designated, varying in character from Victorian

Chancery Lane to post-war high-class suburbia in Downs Hill in an effort to preserve some of the character of the town. These will become increasingly important as housing densities are increased to meet government targets.

Some of the pressure on the use of the swimming baths was relieved by the provision of the West Wickham baths in 1965, one of the last acts of the Beckenham Council. The final transformation came in 1989 when a Leisure Centre was grafted on to produce the building as we know it today. Ten years later the baths themselves were demolished and replaced with a modern building, an integral part of the Spa Leisure Centre. Only the Technical Institute building still remains as a reminder of Beckenham's early enterprise. Now known as 'The Studio', it is used as a council-run arts and media centre.

The policy of acquiring open space has continued with the purchase of South Hill Wood, the 10-acre grounds of a large house near the Bromley border, and the much larger Harvington Estate. Beckenham Place Park, which had been acquired by the London County Council as a public open space in 1928, is since the last boundary change completely in the London Borough of Lewisham, which is currently engaged in a search for a lessee who will maintain it and find an acceptable use for the historic buildings. There can be few towns in the country which have more public parks and open spaces than Beckenham.

156 Tramlink. The new tram terminus at Beckenham Junction. In 2000 the new Tramlink went into service after a long period of teething problems. It ran from Beckenham Junction to Croydon and Wimbledon. Part of its route was along the old disused railway line between Blandford Road and Mackenzie Road.

157   The last day of rail service from Elmers End to Addiscombe.

The writer of the history of any place finds it difficult to draw a line between the past and the present and not to feel some of the excitement and enthusiasm of, and the debt we owe to, those largely forgotten men and women who have created the place in which we live today. This is particularly true of Beckenham and it is our hope that this account will do something to ensure that its identity will endure no matter what the future brings.

Inevitably some aspects have received more attention than others, reflecting to some extent the personal interests of the authors but more often gaps in the record. This is something of which we have become increasingly aware as work on this book went on. Should you be irked by the absence of a reference to something of which you have personal knowledge, we hope you will be spurred by this account to make contact through the publisher. Even better, why not put pen to paper and ensure the preservation of your information by having it published by the Local History Society, whose current address you can obtain from the Local History Section of Bromley Central Library?

Bibliography

Anon, 'St Michael's and All Angels, Souvenir of Completion', 1935

Beaver, P., *The Crystal Palace* (Phillimore, 2nd edn. 1986)

Beckenham Cricket Club Centenary Booklet, 1966

Beckenham & Penge Advertiser

Beckenham & Penge Grammar School 1901-1968

Beckenham Journal

Beckenham Journal, Annuals

Beckenham Journal, Centenary Supplement, 1976

Beckenham Journal, Diamond Jubilee Supplement, 1936

Beckenham Lawn Tennis Tournament, Centenary Booklet, 1986

Beckenham Library staff, *A brief introduction to the history of Beckenham*, Beckenham
  Libraries (undated)

Beckenham U.D.C. and Borough Council Minutes

Blake, L., *Bromley in the Front Line*, published by the author, 2nd edn. (1983)

Blake, L., *Before the War—A portrait of Bromley & District, 1929-1939*, published by
  the author (1985)

Borrowman, R., *Beckenham Past & Present* (1910)

Borough of Beckenham Official Guides

British Red Cross Archives

Bromley Borough Local History Society, various publications

Clark, F.J., *The Story of Christ Church 1876-1926*

Collett, S.W., *Centenary of Beckenham Hospital* (1972)

Copeland, H. Rob., *100 years of change in Beckenham* (1974)

Copeland, H. Rob., collection of newspaper cuttings

Copeland, H. Rob., *The Manors of Old Beckenham* (1967)

Copeland, H. Rob., *The Village of Old Beckenham* (1987)

Godfrey, A., *Old Ordnance Survey Maps: Anerley & Penge* (1868)

Godfrey, A., *Old Ordnance Survey Maps: Beckenham* (1861-71)

Godfrey, A., *Old Ordnance Survey Maps: Bromley* (1861)

Godfrey, A., *Old Ordnance Survey Maps: Crystal Palace* (1871)

Godfrey, A., *Old Ordnance Survey Maps: South Norwood* (1868)

Hasted, E., *The History and Topography of Kent* (1797; part III Beckenham & Bromley
  reprinted. Arcturus Press 1985)

Hayes, Miss A.M., *A School at Elmers End*

Hevey, L., *Shortlands*

Hevey, L., *The Early History of Beckenham* (1994 and 1997)

Hevey, L., *The Story of Elmers End*

Hollman, H.P., *A Hundred Up, the record of the Club, Beckenham 1884-1984*

Inman, E.R., *History of Beckenham Place*, Friends of Beckenham Place newsletters

Knight, J. and Duffield, A., *The Story of St. Mary's—Shortlands* (1926)

London Research Centre, various articles

Maggs, K. and De Athe, P., *The Roman Roads of East Surrey and the Kent Border*, (North Downs Press, 1987)

Manning, P., *The Cators* (private publication)

Manning, P., *Churchyard Memorials of St George's Beckenham* (2001)

Martindale, T.D., *Beckenham and Penge Grammar School 1901-1968*

McInally, M., *History of Minshull House School*

Morgan, Philip (ed.), *Domesday Book, Kent* (Phillimore, 1983)

Motor Sport, various articles

Notley, R., *A Guide to St George's Parish Church, Beckenham* (1985)

Porteous, C., *A History of Christ Church, 1876-1976*

Pullen, D., *Penge* (published by the author, 1990). Contains a complete list of all the remaining legible inscriptions in St George's Churchyard, Beckenham.

Somerville Meikle, J., *St John's Eden Park 1932-1982*

Syme & Duncan Ltd, 1870-1970

Tonkin N., *Marian Vian Diamond Jubilee 1932-1992*

Tonkin, N., *Churchfields School The First 100 Years 1890-1990* (2001)

Tookey, G.W., Collection

Tookey, G.W., 'History of Kelsey Park' (to be published)

Wagstaff, J. and Pullen, D.E. (eds.), *Beckenham—an Anthology* (Historical Association, Bromley and Beckenham, 1984)

Wellcome Foundation Ltd, *One Hundred Years* (1980)

Index

Numbers in **bold** refer to caption page numbers